# HENRY THOREAU
# and JOHN MUIR

## AMONG THE NATIVE AMERICANS

### RICHARD F. FLECK

WESTWINDS
PRESS®

*In memory of my father, J. Keene Fleck (1904–1982),*
*proprietor of Parnassus Bookshop and Reference and*
*Acquisitions Librarian at Princeton University.*

First published in 1985 by Archon Books, an imprint of The Shoe String Press, Inc., Hamden, Connecticut.

Front cover photos: background: iStock.com/© Yarygin; left inset: courtesy of the Library of Congress, LC-USZ61-361; right inset: John Muir at Kern Canyon, John Muir Papers, Holt-Atherton Special Collections, University of the Pacific Library, ©1984 Muir-Hanna Trust.

The illustration of the Stickeen totem pole is from *John of the Mountains*, edited by Linnie Marsh Wolfe. Copyright 1938 by Wanda Muir Hanna. Copyright © renewed 1966 by John Muir Hanna and Ralph Eugene Wolfe. Reprinted by permission of Houghton Mifflin Company.

John Muir's sketch of a Yup'ik girl and the photograph of Muir's notes on the Modoc War are from the John Muir Papers, Holt-Atherton Pacific Center for Western Studies, University of the Pacific. Copyright 1984 Muir-Hanna Trust.

The photograph of an etching depicting Maidu Indians of California burning their dead is from *Ballou's Pictorial* (Boston), 2 May 1857.

Library of Congress Cataloging-in-Publication Data
Fleck, Richard F., 1937-
  Henry Thoreau and John Muir among the Native Americans / Richard F. Fleck.
    pages cm
  Originally published: Hamden, Connecticut : Archon Books, 1985.
  Includes bibliographical references and index.
  ISBN 978-1-941821-46-6 (pbk.)
  1. Muir, John, 1838-1914. 2. Thoreau, Henry David, 1817-1862. 3. Indians of North America. 4. Human ecology—United States. 5. Naturalists—United States—Biography. 6. Authors, American—19th century—Biography. 7. Ecology—Philosophy. I. Title.
  QH31.M9F54 2015
  973.04'97—dc23
                        2014043262

Designed by Vicki Knapton

WestWinds Press® An imprint of

GRAPHIC ARTS
BOOKS®

P.O. Box 56118
Portland, OR 97238-6118
(503) 254-5591
www.graphicartsbooks.com

# CONTENTS

# Acknowledgments

The author expresses his gratitude to the University of Wyoming for granting him sabbatical leave during the fall of 1983 to complete this study. During his examination of the John Muir Papers in Stockton, California, he received friendly cooperation and helpful suggestions from Dr. Ronald Limbaugh, Curator of Archives at the Holt-Atherton Pacific Center for Western Studies at the University of the Pacific, and from his assistant, Kirsten Lewis. Herbert Cahoon, Curator of Manuscripts at the Pierpont Morgan Library, was most cooperative. Professor William Turnbull, former editor of *American Indian Quarterly*, provided constructive suggestions for this manuscript. Acknowledgments are given to the journals *American Indian Quarterly, Research Studies*, and *Studies in Language and Culture* (Japan), in which portions of this study originally appeared. Finally the author wishes to thank his wife, Maura, for her constant encouragement, Eugenia Manuelito for her careful typesetting on the word processor, and Lora Van Renselaar for proofreading and updating the manuscript.

CHAPTER I

# Henry Thoreau's Indian Pathway

## INTRODUCTION

Far above timberline on the misty slopes of Mount Katahdin in September 1846, Henry Thoreau was confronted by a frightening and awesome wilderness which he had never experienced along the shores of Walden Pond. Banks of clouds blew in on Thoreau and naked granite cliffs loomed above. He felt that he stood at the very edge of creation in an unfinished universe. For the first time in his life Thoreau felt shocked at nature. As he wrote in *The Maine Woods*, "Perhaps I most fully realized that this was primeval, untamed, and forever untameable *Nature*."[1] And a bit later he both exclaimed and asked, "Think of our life in nature,—daily to be shown matter, to come in contact with it,—rocks, trees, wind on our cheeks! The *solid* earth! The *actual* world! The *common sense! Contact! Contact!* Who are we? *Where* are we?"[2]

Mount Katahdin confronted Thoreau with an outer wilderness that engendered an inner wilderness of idea which ultimately fostered a psychic integration allowing Thoreau to become spiritually fused with nature. Sherman Paul contends that in Maine Thoreau went spiritually beyond the "Shores of America." Going beyond the shores of the continent is what attracted a young Scottish writer to Thoreau. John Muir's own copy of *The*

*Maine Woods* is highly marked and emendated, particularly the section describing the climb of Mount Katahdin. No wonder! He saw in Thoreau a confirmation of his own conviction that the human spirit has an innate need to wed itself with primal wilderness.

For Thoreau no other human being so effectively integrated himself with his natural environment as the Penobscot Indians. Thoreau wrote that nature has made a thousand revelations to the Indian. He returned to Maine two more times in 1853 and 1857 to learn as much as he could about the Indian way of life, however disrupted it was by the white man. Robert F. Sayre in *Thoreau and the American Indians* contends that Thoreau's contact with the Indian guides Joe Aitteon and Joe Polis enabled him to transcend a savagistic and romantic concept of the Indians.

Civilization, Thoreau observed, was in the 1840s and 1850s in the process of destroying *the Maine woods* for mere short-term gain. He advocated that each town preserve some of this wild country so that its inhabitants might continue to have a restoring spiritual fountain. Thoreau lashed out against the cheap and commercial lumber interests in Maine which gradually gobbled up the Indian's domain. The Indian had more to teach us than the lumberman and his banker.

Through experiencing nature in the raw, through coming to know the Indian, and through years of meditation expressed in writing, Thoreau gained metaphysical insight into the creation itself. For Thoreau the Penobscots in the woods of Maine served as "guides'" not in the physical sense of the word but in Dante's sense of the word. The primal human being of a natural environment can lead the "civilized" human back to realities which only lurk somewhere in the modern subconscious mind so subdued by the complex material concerns of industrial society. If a people who have lived in North America for hundreds of generations before the coming of Europeans have nothing to teach the white man, then who does? There can be no better teacher than the Indian for the mystic lore of an entire continent. True, the Indians of Thoreau's day had been subjugated by Euro-American civilization, but not so much so that they had lost their languages, myths, and mysticism. An alert mind like Thoreau's could readily discern that the sacred source which inspired ancient Indian mythology and religion had not died in Indians like Joe Aitteon and Joe Polis, friends with whom he shared evening campfires in Maine. Thoreau could more easily perceive the "thousand revelations" of nature as a result of his contact with his Indian brethren.

## A LIFETIME PURSUIT

Here is a print still more significant at our doors, the print of a race that has preceded us, and this little symbol that Nature has transmitted to us. Yes, *this* arrowheaded character is probably more ancient than any other, and to my mind it has not been deciphered. Men should not go to New Zealand to write or think of Greece and Rome, nor more to New England. New Earths, new themes expect us.

*Journal, X, P. 118*

From the time the youthful Thoreau listened to local Indian tales told by his townsmen and wandered the fields and woods around Concord in search of arrowheads until his deathbed when he uttered the word "Indian," bachelor Thoreau remained almost obsessed by the primal cultures of America. Somehow he wished to learn everything he could about a way of life that had vanished and was vanishing before his eyes. If he could only gain insight during his life into a people whose origins and very existence stemmed from the mystical depths of nature of this new and awesome continent, then, perhaps, he, as well as his literary audience, could renew themselves during an age when Western civilization had become stagnantly materialistic. This mystical "arrowheaded" character of Indian culture had to be deciphered, not destroyed, so that Euro-American civilization would not obliterate itself with its own expanding, mechanistic bulk.

The Indian's essentially harmonious relationship to his natural environment and his original self-reliance not only gained Thoreau's deep respect but also inspired him to lead a similar life. To be close to nature was to be close to the creation and generative forces of life. "How much more conversant," writes Thoreau in his *Journal*, "was the Indian with any wild animal or plant than we are, and in his language is implied all that intimacy, as much as ours is expressed in our language. How many words in his language about a moose, or birch bark, and the like! The Indian stood nearer to wild nature than we."[3] He strikes a similar note in *A Week on the Concord and Merrimack Rivers*: "By the wary intercourse and aloofness of his dim forest life he preserves his intercourse with his native gods, and is admitted from time to time to a rare and peculiar society with nature."[4]

The American Indian's lifestyle, then, was for Thoreau a confirmation, a paradigm of his own philosophy of living simply and harmoniously in a natural environment. To study this paradigm, he read voluminously on various Indian and Yup'ik cultures, and he became acquainted with Penobscot Indians of Maine and, very late in his short life, the Sioux of Minnesota.[5] They were a people from whom he wanted to learn as much as possible. Whether or not Thoreau was being ironic in the following observation made in his *Journal* is a moot point: "The fact is, the history of the white man is a history of improvement, that of the red man a history of fixed habits of stagnation."[6] Vine Deloria's *Custer Died for Your Sins* makes just this point. Had it not been for the "stagnation," any purely Indian qualities that remain with modern tribes would have been forever lost. Jamake Highwater's *Primal Mind* also celebrates the fixed habits of the Indian which have withstood centuries of Euro-American cultural domination. Western civilization, on the other hand, has long since lost its fixed primal roots because of its "history of improvement"; however, what it has lost is irretrievable. Thoreau did not spend half a lifetime searching for what is primal in humanity if he did not think the loss would be irretrievable.

In his *Journal* Thoreau makes an extremely relevant distinction between the white and red man:

> The constitution of the Indian mind appears to be the very opposite
> to that of the white man. He is acquainted with a different side of

nature. He measures his life by winters, not summers. His year is not measured by the sun, but consists of a certain number of moons, and his moons are measured not by days, but by nights. He has taken hold of the dark side of nature; the white man, the bright side.[7]

Thoreau, a lover of winter, night, and moonlight, and the "dark side of nature," is spiritually closer to an Algonquin than to a European. Certainly his deep immersion in the myth and ethos of the American Indians explains in large part his lifestyle, his thoughts, and his being. Thoreau, who became fond of Indians in his early youth, who spent two years at Walden Pond living in the woods observing nature, and who went on numerous excursions into the wilderness of Maine talking with Penobscots, was indeed following an Indian pathway. He was in direct opposition to the nineteenth-century historian who exhibited as much inhumanity to the Indian as the frontiersman by "wielding a pen instead of a rifle."[8] Interestingly enough, Thoreau precedes modern writers like Francis Jennings who make the exact same point about nineteenth-century historians including Francis Parkman.

Thoreau's personal contact with Indian tribesmen of the woodlands of Maine and Minnesota confirmed his belief that the Indians "seem like a race who have exhausted the secrets of nature, tanned with age, while this young and still fair Saxon slip, on whom the sun has not long shone, is but commencing its career."[9] If Western civilization is to commence a career with North America and all of its mythological mystique, it follows that it must learn much from the various Indian cultures and not subjugate them. Thoreau the writer is a case in point for Carl Jung's contention that the Indian is at the very core of the American psyche. Americans, Jung contends, experience both guilt and fascination for Native Americans.

It is a pity that recent American Indian scholarship, including Jamake Highwater's *Primal Mind* and Thomas E. Sanders and Walter Peek's *Literature of the American Indian*,[10] make no mention of Henry David Thoreau regarding white American philosophy which approaches the interrelated mysticism of American Indians. Sanders and Peek state that the concept of Wah'Kontah . . . is so great an abstraction that the non-Indian has seldom been able to grasp the concept. It is "The Great Mystery," somewhat akin to Ralph Waldo Emerson's concept of the Over-Soul, that transcendental concept derived from Eastern mysticism and chronically misunderstood by American literature students, completely unfamiliar to the great mass of Americans: "The soul knows only the soul; the web of events is the flowing robe in which she is clothed . . . One made of divine teaching is the incarnation of the spirit in a form,—in forms, like my own." (P. 2)

And the editors continue with commentary on Emerson's "Brahma":

A statement of Brahma, the Hindu supreme soul of the universe— the essence of being, uncreated, illimitable, timeless—the poem includes the lines, "When me they fly, I am the wings; / I am the doubter and doubt." That is an approximation of the idea—at least as close an approximation as a Judeo-Christian in the European tradition has come." (Pp. 2–3)

This statement unfortunately ignores the most prominent nineteenth-century Indianist, Henry David Thoreau, who spent twenty years learning all that he could about the Indian to foster his own harmonious and natural pattern of living.

Roderick Nash, in *The Wilderness and the American Mind*, somewhat oversimplifies Thoreau's reaction to Penobscot culture recorded in *The Maine Woods* when he states, "But what he saw in Maine raised questions about the validity of . . . primitivistic assumptions. The Indians appeared to be 'sinister and slouching fellows' who made but a 'coarse and imperfect use . . . of Nature.' The savage was hardly the 'child of nature' he once supposed."[11] This statement ignores the fact that Thoreau returned to Maine two more times with far more positive and glowing commentary, particularly regarding Joe Aitteon and Joe Polis, who were to become his close Indian friends.

Roy Harvey Pearce explains that Thoreau was "searching one assumes, for the means to demonstrate harmony and wholeness to American readers and to set up an example for them." And a bit later he writes, "Savages, in their humanity and their thought, in their harmony and their wholeness, might guide men into the happiness proper to civilization."[12] But Thoreau realized, as seen in such essays as "Civil Disobedience" and a "Plea for Captain John Brown" which he had written while he was getting to know Indians, that civilization was responsible for wars, slavery, and bigotry. Thoreau knew all too well that the civilization of his day was hell-bent on invading and destroying natural harmonies. As Francis Jennings points out in his 1976 book *The Invasion of America, Colonialism, and the Cant of Conquest*, "The invaders of strange continents assumed an innate and absolute superiority over all other peoples because of divine endowment; their descendants would eventually secularize the endowment to claim it from nature instead of God, but would leave its absolute and innate qualities unchanged."[13] Surely Thoreau was realistic enough in his appraisal of US government policies to assume that the Indian, as harmonious as his life may have been, will probably not bring "happiness" to civilization no matter how adept Thoreau's depictions of him were. But if Thoreau could prove that the Indian could bring happiness to his own life, then he would have at least taken the first step in showing the way to harmonious living on Mother Earth. The Indian, then, served Thoreau as a paradigm in an age which was beginning to ignore the spiritual and mystical values of nature.

Numerous scholars including Reginald Cook, John Aldrich Christie, Edwin Fussell, Walter Harding, Albert Keiser, Richard Lebeaux, and Lawrence Willson have had a good bit to say about Thoreau and the Indians or about his Indian manuscripts now collected at the Pierpont Morgan Library. Christie, for instance, believes that to view the Indian manuscripts as unfinished excerpts is to miss "the richer harvest which these resources offered him."[14] Fussell, in his essay "The Red Face of Man" (later incorporated in his book *Frontier: American Literature and the American West*), sadly comes to the conclusion that Thoreau viewed the Indian as a lower-scale development of the modern man with little or no art or abstract aesthetic expression: Thoreau came to the realization, believes Fussell, that "The Indian's inability to express himself in art . . . has caused his extinction"![15] Two more recent works, my own *The Indians of Thoreau* and Robert F. Sayre's *Thoreau and the American Indians*, have helped to bring to the forefront a clearer understanding, I hope, of the nature of Thoreau's interest in American Indian cultures.

## THE INDIAN NOTEBOOKS

Just what were Thoreau's interests, and how did they manifest themselves in his thought? A clear understanding of the Indian notebooks or Indian books now in New York City is necessary. Robert Sayre points out that the Indian notebooks or Extracts Concerning the Indians or Indian books are a pathway over a fourteen-year period along which Thoreau leads himself out of an inadequate savagistic notion of Indian cultures to a more mature, realistic understanding of the complexities of American Indian tribalism. Sayre writes in his preface that "The 'Indian Books' and trips to Maine also took him, to some degree, beyond savagism," and later in the book he explains how Thoreau got beyond savagism: "Yet as Henry came to recognize the amazing social qualities of Indians, both from his reading and his times in Maine, the image of 'the Indian' as solitary rebel had to give way."[16] But I feel that the notebooks reflect Thoreau's intuitive or spiritual interests in Indian cultures which were not necessarily more "savagistic" in his earlier writings than in his mature writings but which were less spiritually developed when he wrote *A Week on the Concord and Merrimack Rivers* in 1845–47. As he culled his facts on Indians, his spiritual philosophy of living evolved. Individual facts fueled his spiritual and transcendental overviews expressed in *Walden*, which, as we know, was written and rewritten many times after his departure from the pond. All the while he kept studying the Indian.

These voluminous Indian books in Thoreau's hand consist of 2,800 pages in eleven volumes now housed in the Pierpont Morgan Library. They are under lock and key and contained in Morocco leather slipcases and were considered to be of such value that during World War II, when there existed the potential threat of Nazi buzz bombing, they were removed from New York and kept in Albany until the war was over. The Indian books were started in 1847 while Thoreau was still in his cabin at Walden Pond, because we know he composed most of *A Week on the Concord and Merrimack Rivers* while still at Walden Pond. In volume I of the Indian books on the fortieth page, we find the following notation from Thomas Hutchinson's *History of the Colony of Massachusetts Bay*:

> God was Ketan—gave man fair weather. Powwows caused sickness—Passaconaway made them believe that he could make water burn, rocks move, and trees dance, and metamorphose himself into a flaming man; that in winter he could raise a green leaf out of the ashes of a dying one, and produce a living snake from the skin of a dead one.

Thoreau found this bit of a note to be of enough significance to include in Wednesday of *A Week*, which describes the wise old Indian Sachem Passaconaway, who restrained his people from going to war with the English and performed miracles which Thoreau does not question. This portion of *A Week* was written while at Walden Pond but toward the end of his two-year stay. So the notebooks were begun sometime in 1847. The relatively short first volume was followed by ten more much larger books, some of which were over three hundred handwritten pages as opposed to a thin notebook kept at Walden of less than one hundred pages. He had started a habit which he couldn't control—taking notes and more notes on Indian cultures of North and South America and eventually on all aboriginal peoples of the world. And while he took notes he also developed his philosophy of living simply and closely to the natural world. In *Walden*, for instance, he states that a wigwam is a superior dwelling compared with the fancy home of the white man.

One of the two most significant works that appears throughout all eleven volumes is Henry Roe Schoolcraft's *Historical and Statistical Information Respecting the History, Condition and Prospects of the Indian Tribes of the United States* in six volumes 1851–57. This is one of the most impressive governmental studies written under the auspices of the Bureau of Indian Affairs. Schoolcraft, married to an Indian woman, states in his preface, "With all their defects of character, the Indian tribes are entitled to the peculiar notice of a people who have succeeded to the occupancy of territories which once belonged to them. They constitute a branch of the human race whose history is lost in the early and wild mutations of men."[17]

The other important source for Thoreau was the multivolumed *Jesuit Relations* (1632–73) in French written as firsthand accounts of essentially pre-Columbian myths, legends, and lifestyles before the Christianization process. Such Jesuits as Sebastien Rasles and Fathers Le Jeune and Le Mercier gave Thoreau tremendous insight into tribal customs and practices before white corruption. Their directness and simplicity of style were, I am sure, refreshing to the reader Henry David Thoreau. All of his notes were taken in French, and some of them found their way into his writings in translated form. *The Jesuit Relations* and Schoolcraft's *History*, though written by whites with obvious prejudices, did give Thoreau a rich harvest of cultural data both of a religious and secular order.

Some of the other important books he culled information from about North America were William Bartram's *Travels Through North and South Carolina*, Jonathan Carver's *Three Years' Travel Through the Interior Parts of North America*, David Crantz's *History of Greenland*, John Heckewelder's *Account of the History, Manners and Customs of the Indian Nations*, Peter Kalm's *Travels Into North America*, Alexander Mackenzie's *Voyages from Montreal*, and John Tanner's fascinating *Narrative of Captivity*. However, Thoreau, as he took notes on American Indian cultures, branched out to other tribal cultures of the world. On Polynesian cultures, he got information from James Cook's *Journal* (as did Mark Twain for his book *Roughing It*) and on African cultures from David Livingstone's *Travels in South Africa*. As John Aldrich Christie contends, Thoreau was indeed a world traveler, and the Indian manuscripts certainly serve as a case in point. Additionally, he made notes on Australian bushmen, on Arabian Bedouins, and of course on all cultures of the polar regions. He was fascinated by prehistoric Celts and Norsemen, and by the 1850s was busy digesting information on ancient Scandinavia from Laing's *Journal of Residence in Norway*. Clearly he sought information about primal living throughout the planet.

Certainly the North American Indian cultures from the eastern woodlands to the Southwest were of immense interest to Thoreau; but equally important were all ancient races when mankind was part of a common ethos on a one-to-one basis with the planet, and when we did not rely on artificial removes or mere extensions of ourselves via electricity, steam power, nuclear power, or whatever. The reenacted voyages of the *Kon Tiki*, the RA expedition, and Saint Brendan the Navigator link our own age's intrigue with primal man to that of Thoreau's. Thoreau, Highwater, Deloria, Heyerdahl all search for a basic commonality among primal peoples living in nature.

What did Thoreau record during those fourteen years between 1847 and 1861? The following is a list of topics Thoreau jotted down at the end of his first Indian book: traveling, physique, music, games, dwellings, feasting, food, charity, funeral customs, tradition and history, morale, marriage customs, manufacturers, education, dress, painting, money, naming, government, treatment of captives, mariners, woodcraft, hunting, fishing, superstitions and religions, medicine, war, language, Indian relics, and finally arts derived from the Indians. By the middle of his note-taking process he began to categorize his notes; his notes became more organized. The two categories of traditions and history and religion and superstition are by far the most dominant throughout the eleven books. The other more factual categories of notes on pottery, sexual mores, weapons, etc., while important, represent a combined total of 50 or 55 percent. In other words, twenty-eight categories take up only about half the total and two categories take up about 45 percent of the notes. A closer examination of these categories will follow.

Still another kind of material contained in these manuscripts is tiny bits of commentary, one- or two-line reactions of Thoreau to the material he is extracting. While some of these reactions are barely worth mentioning, others are of considerable importance. After reading David Crantz's *History of Greenland*, for instance, Thoreau noted, "I am struck by the close resemblance in manners and customs of Greenlanders and our Indian. If they are proved to be a distinct race—it will show that similarity of manners and customs is no evidence of a common origin."[18] Here we get back to that commonality of a natural lifestyle. Vine Deloria states in *Custer Died for Your Sins* that if Druidic white people came to America when they were still a communal, tribalistic culture, the American Indians would have been their soul brothers. However, post-Roman Europeans with analytical, nonintuitive minds were on a cultural collision course with Woodland and Plains Indian cultures. But not Henry David Thoreau!

Yet another piece of material in the Indian books is a fragmentary essay linking together Indians with ancient Europeans (see appendix). Because of this brief essay and because these notebooks were kept right up to his illness in 1861, I believe had Thoreau lived long enough, he would probably have written a book or series of essays on the Indians. True enough, as Sayre points out, a modest amount (perhaps 5 to 7 percent) of the notebook material found its way into his *Journal* and *Walden* and *The Maine Woods*, and, Sayre notes, *The Maine Woods* is after all his true Indian book.

But *The Maine Woods* is far more than an Indian book. It is a forceful social critique as well as a metaphysical treatise on the nature of nature. *The Maine Woods* is not just his Indian book; I beg to differ with Robert Sayre. If I may intuit a bit myself from the viewpoint of being a creative writer, eventually a good deal of note material finds itself in one's writing once one knows why and for what purpose he or she is taking notes. It might take ten years for a germinal idea to surface; but what is always amazing to the writer is that the germ of an idea, unrecognizable as it may be in its initial form, will take shape, somehow, in the future (unless the writer is completely irresponsible or alcoholic à la Harry in Hemingway's *Snows of Kilimanjaro*). The fact that some 90 percent of the *Indian Notebooks* remains unused from a literary standpoint forces me to conclude that the Indian books would have filtered into more of pure Thoreau either in more books relating to the Indian as *The Maine Woods* or indeed by further reflection on an alternate lifestyle in the midst of a roaring Industrial Revolution. In other words, a writer's ambitious energy usually gets the job done unless ill health or death obviously disrupts the process.

Thoreau was searching for commonalities while keeping in mind differences between civilizations and "savage" states. One basic commonality of all primal cultures throughout the planet is the drum or tambour. "There would appear to be a kind of necessity in human nature to produce this instrument," writes Thoreau, and it is very significant that this piece of antique heritage can be heard in London and Paris thousands of years later.[19] Another commonality linking white people of Europe with the Indian of North America is the age prior to the use of metals where stone spearpoints were used around the globe—that age when Vine Deloria suggests all men were soul brothers in their lifestyle. Thoreau makes special note of King Sigfried, who imposed a duty on his people of five missile stones to be brought to his castle. That age before the use of metal, as Lawrence Willson notes in his doctoral dissertation, was perhaps the most fascinating for Thoreau.[20] For not only were people's lifestyles similar but also their collective myths and religions. Each living thing of nature had a sacred significance to all people of the globe; all things were, so to speak, symbols of spiritual facts, and nowhere better can this be seen than in the strikingly similar ancient creation myths, flood myths, and etiological or phenomena tales. More of this later.

Thoreau was not so Romantic and idealistic in his appreciation of the Indian that he failed to see anything wrong. He was well aware that the atrocities of Indians were as savage as those of the Persians of the mid-nineteenth century. He was aware of torture practices of woodland tribes. Cruelty was and is a negative commonality linking all people of all times.

In addition to bits of original Thoreauvian commentary such as "the mythology of Asia present everywhere in North America" (i.e., the tortoise myth of ancient Hindus and the turtle myth of the Hurons), there are a few notes of Thoreau as reminders to seek out yet other sources such as the Indian poems of Philip Freneau. Some of the excerpts Thoreau made, while not developed in fragmentary essays, were eventually incorporated into such works as *A Week on the Concord and Merrimack Rivers*, as I have already shown, as well as *Walden*, *The Maine Woods*, and the *Journal*. All of this strongly suggests that he wasn't addicted to note taking for the sake of it—these notebooks are, indeed, more than mere antiquarian curiosa, as one publisher informed me before I was successful in procuring a press for edited selections.

But let us turn briefly to the twenty-eight categories of notes which comprise 55 percent of the manuscripts and then more extensively to the other two categories of myths and religions—that grand commonality— which make up almost half of the *Indian Notebooks*.

Thoreau's notes of customs and practices of Indians plus his observations of Penobscot culture in Maine buttressed his own desires to be self-reliant in the natural world of North America. He writes in his *Journal* on 20 March 1858, "Suppose they [Indians] had generally become the laboring class among the whites that my father had been a farmer and had an Indian for his hired man, how many aboriginal ways we children should have learned from them."[21] And later on 3 February 1859 he muses:

> If wild men, so much more like ourselves than they are unlike, have inhabited these shores before us, we wish to know particularly what manner of men they were, how they lived here, their relations to nature, their arts and their customs, their fancies and superstitions. They paddled over these waters, they wandered in these woods.[22]

In short, because these people lived in North America for thousands of years, it behooves Americans who expect to live there thousands of years more to try to learn of their ways. In a sense the architecture of American minds can be more quickly shaped by studying the ways of these people.

Americans have no link with the remote past on their continent. Indians could become the Americans' grandparents as indeed they do for Tom Outland in Willa Cather's novel, *The Professor's House*.

After Thoreau had met members of the Penobscot tribe in 1846 and again in 1853 and 1857, he became increasingly fascinated with Indian woodcraft, fishing and hunting, burial practices, and other things. *The Maine Woods* commences with a reactionary, almost puritanical tone toward the Indians; Thoreau was experiencing culture shock. But after he returned several years later to meet Joe Aitteon and Joe Polis, whom he respected as individuals, he was able to appreciate in a liberated fashion such things as canoe building, woodcraft, and, above all, the language and humanity of the Indians. Thoreau, deep in the spruce- and moose-filled woods of Maine, gained appreciation for the Indian's humanity through his keen sense of humor. As Thoreau observed with another traveling companion, Joe Polis (whom Richard Lebeaux describes as a kind of surrogate brother), he noted that he set himself up as a debating judge by saying, "you beat"—"he beat." Or when one of the white men remarked to Polis that he saw that he had not stretched his moose hides out to dry, the Indian remarked, "What you ask me that question for? Suppose I stretch 'em, you see 'em? Maybe your way of talking . . . no Indian way."[23] One can imagine the gleam in Thoreau's eye.

An interesting parallel can be drawn between Thoreau and his admirer, John Muir. Muir, too, expressed an almost puritanical "uptight" feeling when he first met Tlingit (pronounced Klinkit) Indians of Panhandle Alaska. But once he got to know individual Indians like Toyatte, described in *Travels in Alaska*, Muir overcame his cultural prejudices and became fascinated at first with their totem poles, lodges, and woodcraft and eventually their myths and legends and philosophy. Of course Muir's Indian education was less bookish than Thoreau's. A parallel between *The Maine Woods* and *Travels in Alaska* will be drawn later in this study.

All during and between Thoreau's voyages to the Maine woods, the *Indian Notebooks* grew and grew. Throughout the 1850s Thoreau made sketches of such things as kayaks, canoes, pottery, wigwams, and burial posts of the northeastern woodland tribes. And out west, Thoreau notes from Maximillian that "Among the Blackfeet, the dead are not buried in the ground, if it can be avoided. The body is sewn up in a buffalo robe,

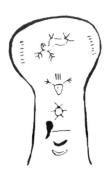

dressed in his best clothes, his face painted red, but without his weapons, and laid in some retired place in ravines, rocks, forests, or high steep banks" (VII, MA 602, P. 38). Being sewn up in a buffalo robe for Thoreau, I would imagine, is a most mystical expression of man's mergence with nature.

All through Thoreau's *Journal* as well as in his Indian manuscripts are sketches of such things as Indian beaver traps and fish weirs. From Thomas Hutchinson's *History of the Colony of Massachusetts Bay*, Thoreau, while still at Walden Pond, extracted the following:

I have seen a Native go into the woods with his hatchet, carrying only a basket of corn with him, and stones to strike a fire. When he had felled his tree (being a chestnut) he made him a little house or shed of the bark of it; he [makes] fire . . . his corn he boils, and hath and brook by him, and sometimes angles for a little fish . . . Within ten or twelve days . . . finished his boat; with which afterwards he ventures out to fish the ocean. (I, MA 596, P. 37)

As he copied this down in his own wooden hut, I believe he must have felt his lifestyle at least approximated the Indian's. Certainly Joe Polis, the woodsman who could make torches out of birch bark and who could handle a canoe as well as he could walk, was a living confirmation of his earlier note from Hutchinson. Polis educated Thoreau in wild foods of the Maine woods, and his Indian manuscripts are filled with notes on Indian food and drink such as milk from tame deer, cider from wild apples, pumpkins, squash, cranberries, potage, fish and wild game, raspberries, blueberries, and combination of fruit and meat pounded into a cake.

The Indian mode of travel on snowshoes through the snowy wood-lands and in kayaks through cold waters and soft deer skin moccasins in dry woodlands was to Thoreau vastly superior to the British pegged boot. He comments in *A Yankee in Canada* on how the Canadians wisely learned to emulate the ways of the Indian for traveling through wilder-ness. The English colonists of America vainly clung to ways of the Old World. Many a squadron of British soldiers, refusing to wear snowshoes, was wiped out by the Iroquois during winters of the French-Indian Wars because the Indian was on top of the snow while the British remained waist deep.

Thoreau was fascinated by Indian names for things and places, as is readily seen in *The Maine Woods* by his constant questioning of Polis for words for this thing and that. In the notebooks he jotted down the name of Philadelphia—*Kuejjnenaku*—the grove of long pines. And, as Thoreau discovered, contrary to what the modern folklorist Stith Thompson con-tends, the American Indians had many names for stars and atmospheric phenomena: "The Aurora Borealis is 'The dance of the dead' and 'Milky Way' is called the 'Bath of Souls'" (III, MA 598, P. 89).

Indian language had great significance for Thoreau. Any book which contained American Indian vocabulary was to Thoreau of great interest. Two books of particular significance to him were Alexander Mackenzie's *Voyages From Montreal*, which contains lists of words in three columns; the word is given in English with its Knisteneaux and Algonquin equivalents. Thoreau copied down these vocabulary tables and probably attempted some memorization. The other book Thoreau discovered was *Father Rasles' Dictionary of the Abenaki Language* from which Thoreau jot-ted down fourteen pages word for word. In his *Journal* dated 5 March 1858 Thoreau writes:

A dictionary of the Indian language reveals another and wholly new life to us. Look at the word 'wigwam' and see how close it brings you to the ground . . . It reveals to me a life within a life, or rather a life without a life, as it were threading the woods between our towns still, and yet we can never tread in its trail. The Indian's earthly life was far off from us as heaven is.[24]

By the time we get to the last essay of Thoreau's in *The Maine Woods*, we see a fascination for Penobscot vocabulary. Thoreau constantly asks Polis for Indian equivalents of natural objects; for example, when Thoreau asked the translation for wild lily bulbs which were being prepared for soup, he was told *Sheepnoc*.

An original comment from Thoreau's volume one of the *Indian Notebooks* links the Indian's concept of language with his own: "The eloquent savage indulges in tropes and metaphors—he uses nature as a symbol . . . his metaphors are not far fetched—into his speech. He looks around him in the woods . . . to aid his expression. His language though more flowery is less artificial" (I, MA 596, P. 17). As Thoreau notes, "What they have a word for they have a thing for," and a little later in the same volume of the *Journal* he writes, "It is an advantage if words [are] derived originally from nature."[25]

Nowhere is this idea more apparent than in hieroglyphs. Thoreau's notes from Schoolcraft on hieroglyphs are exhaustive. He copied down, for instance, some hieroglyphs of the Algonquin people called Ke-Ke-no-win, or the highest grade of the symbolic. These hieroglyphs mean "I am rising," "I take the sky," "I walk through the sky," and "The Eastern Woman calls (Venus)."[26]

It is a pity Thoreau could not have traveled to the West to see the many sandstone petroglyphs, one set of which were explained to me as being supernatural. Far back in the canyon country of Wind River Indian

Reservation in Wyoming, I was shown one of these petroglyphs at sunset and was told that anyone seeking medicine should come here after fasting and bathing. You would hear voices from afar at sundown but they were really near. After you lost consciousness, you would see the veins of the earth throbbing; each vein represented a disease of mankind which could be cured by various plants which the Great Spirit would show. You would know the Great Spirit had spoken by awakening the next morning, seemingly only minutes later, with an eagle plume in your lap. All of this is represented in the various petroglyphs behind your back. I do not know how much more earthly and heavenly you can get than that. Petroglyphs and hieroglyphs are indeed translations of natural phenomena into language. But it is the language of myth expressing universal human truths of primal man in nature that Thoreau seems to be most enticed by as evidenced by its overwhelming predominance throughout the eleven manuscript volumes on the Indians. Let us now turn to the myths themselves.

## INDIAN MYTHOLOGY

Primal man living within a rain forest or an arid plain or on alpine heights remains completely open to the forces of nature whether in the form of volcanoes, tornadoes, or gentle mist rising from a bog. These generative forces evoke within him the desire to mythologize, to tell stories of fellow man within the midst of his wild world. Through the years from the 1840s to the late 1850s, Thoreau's fascination with primal mythology grew steadily. He theorized that the pure wilderness, particularly such phenomena as mist rising from the sea or lakes, engendered myth. Inasmuch as he himself created mythic passages in *Walden* involving mist (looking like some nocturnal conventicle), it is clear to see why Indian mist myths would have quickly gained his attention. One such myth caught his eye while reading through Thomas Hutchinson when he was still at the pond:

> In former times, a great many moons ago, a bird, extraordinary
> for its size used often to visit the south shore of Cape Cod, and

carry from thence to the Southward, a vast number of small children. Maushop, who was an Ind. Giant, as fame reports, resided
in these parts. Enraged at the loss of many of the children he, on
a certain time, waded into the sea in pursuit of the bird till he
had crossed the sound and reached Nantucket. Before Maushop
forded the sound, the island was unknown to the aborigines of
America. Tradition says, that Maushop found the bones of the
children in a heap under a huge tree. He then wishing to smoke a
pipe, searched the island for tobacco; but finding none, filled his
pipe with poke a weed which the Ind. sometimes used as its sub-
stitute. Ever since the above men[tioned] memorable event, fogs
have been frequent at Nantucket even the Cape. In allusion to this
tradition when the aborigines observed a fog rising they would
say, "there comes old Maushop's smoke." (I, MA 596, P. 77)

While this jotting did not get into *Cape Cod*, he did add it to his *Journal* on
20 June 1857.[27]

Mist and fog are forces capable of producing anthropomorphic
shapes and forms, and this generative aspect of nature in turn generates
myths. Both Thoreau and his ancient predecessors are one in their appreciation of the generative forces of which Thoreau sings praises in "Spring"
of *Walden*. He jotted down scores of Indian praises of creation which, I am
sure, had he lived, would have found their way into his writings. If Americans are to commence their existence with North America having lost contact with Celtic, Druidic, or Nordic gods, it follows that they must learn of
the new continent's mythological mystique as seen through the eyes of its
fifty-thousand-years-old inhabitants.

I believe that an important part of Thoreau's purpose in writing his
2,800 handwritten pages of the Indian books was to write a book or series
of essays on North American Indians which would correct the myopic
view of nineteenth-century Euro-American historians by giving them for
the first time a *North American's* appreciation of his own continent which
was and is rich in mythology. Indian myths generated out of the primal

forces of nature would have played an important role in his book. The fact that the Indian, like Thoreau, saw the Great Spirit in everything leads me to believe that he was a relativist and like Claude Levi-Strauss, in his *Structural Anthropology and The Naked Man*, believed that mythological unities existed among varied tribal groups beyond the shores of America. As civilization progressed and gradually shielded Europeans from their Druidic beliefs in the importance of sacredness of certain trees such as the oak, the hazel, and the linden, or shielded Europeans from their one-to-one relationship with Mother Earth, they began to lose their mythic links with other tribesmen. Thoreau, above all, sought that unity, and his study of American Indian myths, however garbled his sources were as Sayre contends, helped him see human unity through a commonality of natural experience.

The deeper Thoreau immersed himself into Indian mythologies both by reading and visiting the Penobscots and later the Sioux, the more Thoreau realized their richness of expression, for mythology is indeed another word for history. Through it we can see ourselves better and through the American Indian, we can see North America in us more clearly. Frank Waters, author of *The Book of the Hopi*, contends that the land, after many human generations, shapes the psyche and that pure Europeans eventually will become Indian in features and thought. As the American wilderness enters our myths, we are meeting the expectation of the land. Thoreau, in traveling along the trail of the Indian, more than met the expectations of the land; he beckoned us to do the same. His kinship with the American Indian was as complete as possible for a nineteenth-century white man as he readily accepted their wisdom and lifestyle which grew out of living essentially harmoniously for thousands of years in North America.

Nature lies at the root of Thoreau's concept of mythology as it does for his transcendental philosophy. "Nature," he writes in "Natural History of Massachusetts," "is mythical and mystical always."[28] The very Indian ground upon which Thoreau trod in northern Maine inspired him to write, "I looked with awe . . . to see what the powers had made there, the form and fashion and material for their work. This was the Earth of which we have heard, made out of Chaos and Old Night."[29] We can see Thoreau's mind working backward; that is, his present response to his surroundings, because they are primal, is intuitively assumed to be a timeless, universal one. As nature is for Thoreau, so it must have been for the ancients. The wilderness, be it in the form of starlit skies, forests, wild animals, or rugged mountains, is of fundamental importance, Thoreau assumes, in the formation of early American Indian folktales and myths. It is responsible for, as Thoreau notes from Henry Roe Schoolcraft in the unpublished *Indian Notebooks*, the richly varied tradition of

> nations creeping out of the ground—a world growing out of a tortoise's back—the globe reconstructed from the earth clutched in a muskrat's paw after the deluge. A mammoth bull jumping over the great lakes; a grape-vine carrying a whole tribe across the Mississippi; an eagle's wings producing the phenomenon of thunder, on its flashing eyes that of lightning; men stepping in viewless tracks of the blue arch of heaven; the rainbow made a baldric; a little boy catching the sun's beams in a wave; hawks rescuing ship wrecked mariners from an angry ocean, and carrying them up a steep ascent in leather bags. (V, MA 600, Pp. 53–54)

John Muir would come to a similar acceptance of the Indian's environmental harmony, though less from reading and more from experience with Native Americans. Both Thoreau and Muir sensed an inexorable bond with the Creator through the Indian in his wilderness, but tribal languages do not contain the word *wilderness* simply because wilderness is home, and so it was for Henry Thoreau, (at the very least, spiritually), and for John Muir.

## CHAPTER II

# John Muir's Homage to Henry David Thoreau

IN WILDNESS IS THE PRESERVATION
OF THE WORLD.
HENRY DAVID THOREAU

IN GOD'S WILDNESS LIES THE
HOPE OF THE WORLD.
JOHN MUIR

Though John Muir never met Henry David Thoreau in person, he was indebted to him as his spiritual and literary mentor. The closest their paths came to crossing came in the spring of 1861 when Thoreau traveled to Minnesota via the Mississippi River from East Dubuque, Illinois, past Prairie du Chien, Wisconsin, to Fountain City, Wisconsin, and St. Paul, Minnesota. Thoreau took the trip in a vain effort to improve his ailing lungs and, as Walter Harding notes, to study American Indian cultures and American flora and fauna.[1] Thoreau's return trip took him in late June 1861 back to Prairie du Chien and by rail to Milwaukee and a Great Lakes passage to upstate New York.

During this same period, from May to June 1861, John Muir had left the University of Wisconsin in Madison to return home for his summer holidays at the Muir farm at Hickory Hill not far from Portage, Wisconsin. I suppose Thoreau and Muir were but fifty miles apart when Thoreau rode the train from Prairie du Chien to Milwaukee on 26 June 1861. (It is even possible that they unknowingly crossed paths in Madison, according to Edmund A. Schofield in his article "Muir and the New England Connection.") By this time Muir had certainly heard of Thoreau; but it was not until 1862, the year of Thoreau's death, that Muir became acquainted with some writings of Thoreau and Emerson at the home library of his geology professor, Ezra Slocum Carr. According to Linnie Marsh Wolfe, Muir was led to read Emerson's essays "The American Scholar" and "Nature." On the professor's shelves were, in all probability, a copy of *Walden* and *A Week on the Concord and Merrimack Rivers*. Mrs. Carr quite frequently discussed the writings of Emerson and Thoreau with young John Muir.

While Muir was barely beginning his career in 1861, Thoreau was ending his. As a result of his Minnesota journey, Thoreau further revised one of his most striking lectures, "Wild Apples" (which was finally published the year of his death), and he took more notes on Indian cultures based upon his brief visit to the Lower Sioux Agency at Fort Ridgely, Minnesota. Thoreau had completed, as best as possible, his Indian education which began in 1847 at Walden Pond when he commenced his *Indian Notebook* project and when he first visited the Maine woods which afforded him the unique opportunity of befriending Penobscot Indians. This education continued through the 1850s until his Minnesota journey in 1861. A dying Henry Thoreau was able to see his first Indian dances, including a Sioux Dream Dance.[2] Though his notes are sparse, one can only assume that these people deeply touched Thoreau's spirit. For Thoreau, the Indian was a key to understanding North America, and for Muir, the Indian was a key to living in harmony with our new continent.

John Muir's battles and struggles for conserving Yosemite and the Hetch Hetchy drained him of all of his spiritual energies, as Stephen Fox so well describes in his recent book *John Muir and His Legacy*. For him to have been able to write such forceful essays as "The American Forests" in *Our National Parks* is more than a tribute to his miraculous reserve strength.

Duties at his ranch in Martinez of raising fruit crops and preserving them for shipment occupied much of his energies during the 1880s. Naturally he did this out of devotion for his beloved wife and daughters. Louie, the ideal wife for John Muir, sensed when his energies were drained and insisted he go off to the wilderness of Mount Rainier or Alaska to renew his spirit and mind. Between excursions to the wild from 1894 to 1914, Muir was a busy beaver in his "scribble den" at Martinez where he wrote seven books for publication and countless thousands of letters, notes, journal entries, essays, aphorisms, and an autobiography which largely became incorporated in *Boyhood and Youth* and *Travels in Alaska*. One need only look at the index of unpublished materials at the Holt-Atherton Pacific Center for Western Studies (now called the John Muir Center) to see that Muir's writing activities were phenomenal to say the least.

With the exception of *The Mountains of California* and *Our National Parks*, all of Muir's books were written under the influence of Henry David Thoreau. Why do I make this contention? In 1906 John Muir wrote to Herbert Gleason to ask him to ask Houghton Mifflin to send to Martinez the twenty-volume Riverside set of the writings of Henry David Thoreau. Finally in 1907 the set was delivered to John Muir, who proceeded to read it voraciously. Keep in mind that Muir, of course, had already read *Walden* (probably back at Madison in 1862) and *The Maine Woods* by 1870 (he refers to it in a letter to Mrs. Ezra S. Carr dated 29 May 1870). Muir dedicated himself to twenty years of writing and in the process felt he needed a philosophical and literary guide. Henry Thoreau was his answer.[3]

What does one find in examining John Muir's personal set of the writings of Henry David Thoreau? The most obvious thing is a handwritten index at the back of each volume. At the back of volume III, *The Maine Woods*, for instance, Muir has written in pencil various topics of interest with page references. Among these topics are "Indians." If one goes to the text of each of the volumes, he will find underlinings, vertical lines, and occasional marginalia consisting of Muir's reaction to Thoreau. All of these markings give us a clear indication that John Muir carefully read Henry Thoreau cover to cover.

In "The American Forests," a diatribe against the foolish government support of lumber interests, Muir invokes the name of Thoreau once again:

> Travelers through the West in summer are not likely to forget the firework display along the various railway tracks. Thoreau, when contemplating the destruction of the forests on the east side of the continent, said that soon the country would be so bald that every man would have to grow whiskers to hide its nakedness, but he thanked God that at least the sky was safe. Had he gone West he would have found out that the sky was not safe; for all through the summer months, over most of the mountain regions, the smoke of mill and forest fires is so thick and black that no sunbeam can pierce it.[4]

The government must step in to protect trees, God's gift to humanity. As Thoreau is critical of the misuse of trees in Maine ("Think how stood the white-pine tree on the shore of Chesuncook, its branches with the four winds, and every individual needle trembling in the sunlight—think how it stands with it now—sold, perchance, to the New England Friction-Match Company!")[5], Muir lashes out with equally strong irony: "The laborious vandals had seen 'the biggest tree in the world,' then forsooth, they must try to see the biggest stump and dance on it."[6] The most significant part of the destruction of the wilderness is not necessarily of the trees but of the people of the wilderness, the American Indians. Nothing is worse for Thoreau and Muir than a *degraded* Indian. Thoreau writes in *The Maine Woods* that "There is, in fact, a remarkable and unexpected resemblance between the degraded savage and the lowest classes in a great city. The one is no more a child of nature than the other."[7] Muir was equally perturbed with some of the Indians of the California mountains:

> Presently the English-speaking shepherd came in, to whom I explained my wants and what I was doing. Like most white men, he could not conceive how anything other than gold could be the

object of such rambles as mine, and asked repeatedly whether I had discovered any mines. I tried to make him talk about trees and the wild animals, but unfortunately he proved to be a tame Indian from the Tule Reservation, had been to school, claimed to be civilized, and spoke contemptuously of "Wild Indians," and so of course his inherited instincts were blurred or lost.[8]

The very thing Muir sought in the wilderness this Indian had lost. As Roy Harvey Pearce points out in his book *The Savages of America: A Study of the Indian and the Idea of Civilization*, it was not that primitivists like Thoreau and Muir wanted to do away with civilization, but that civilized men should have the integrity of the Indian.

John Muir was no rote imitator of Thoreau but rather a thoughtful integrator of this New England master into his own system of Sierra values. He read and digested Thoreau, but energies coming out of this process had the distinct quality of John Muir. Were it not for Muir's deep literary appreciation of the writing of Henry David Thoreau, perhaps he would have never really overcome his difficulty with, as he put it, "dead bone heaps of words."[9] Henry Thoreau gave him the inspiration to express his own unique feelings, thoughts, and observations coming from experience that Thoreau could have never even dreamed of: climbing high, windy Mount Shasta to be trapped by a blizzard and frozen and volcanically roasted for one perilous night; or looking into the high Himalaya Mountains from the deodar forests of India; or bouncing along a rough Arctic glacier in a dogsled driven by a Siberian Chukchi native; or camping in the high Sierra with a US president and succeeding in conveying to him the need for a national park system. John Muir gained, I venture to say, immeasurable literary skills and enjoyment by reading Thoreau. But were Thoreau able to read such books as Muir's *Travels in Alaska* or *My First Summer in the Sierra*, who can say what may have been the effect on his life!

Though young John Muir missed Thoreau by fifty miles back in Wisconsin in June 1861, he did get to see Thoreau's old haunts in June 1893. He visited Sleepy Hollow Cemetery and laid flowers on Thoreau's and Emerson's graves. "I think it is the most beautiful graveyard I ever saw," writes Muir.[10] After leaving his beloved Henry Thoreau, he walked through the woods to Walden Pond. He reflected that this was "a beautiful lake . . . fairly embosomed like a bright dark eye in wooded hills of smooth moraine of gravel and sand, and with a rich leafy undergrowth of huckleberry, willow, and young oak bushes." And Muir adds, "No wonder Thoreau lived here two years. I could have enjoyed living here two hundred or two thousand . . . how people should regard Thoreau as a hermit on account of his little delightful stay here I cannot guess."[11] That evening Muir dined with Emerson's son, Edward Waldo Emerson and, of all people, Edward's father-in-law who was a college mate of Thoreau! Surely, years later, Muir read his 1906 edition of *Walden* back at Martinez with more intimacy than ever before. The spirit of Thoreau must have touched him deeply during his exhaustive writing days after 1907. As Penobscots had taught Thoreau much about woodlore, so, too, had they taught Muir much about living harmoniously in the forests as did a young McCloud River Indian (Winnemem Wintu) boy instruct young Muir that saxifrage was a tasty plant to eat. When Muir's own day came to an end on Christmas Eve, 1914, Alaska was very much on his mind. While he may not have uttered the word "Indian" just before he died as Thoreau reportedly had done, John Muir was certainly *thinking* about Indians and Yup'iks of the Alaskan Arctic.

CHAPTER III

## John Muir Among the Maidu,
## Tlingit, and Yup'ik People

INTRODUCTION

Thus, by forces seemingly antagonistic and destructive, has
Mother Nature accomplished her beneficent designs—now a flood
of fire, now a flood of ice, now a flood of water: and at length an
outburst of organic life, a milky way of snowy petals and wings,
girdling the rugged mountain like a cloud, as if the vivifying sunbeams beating against its sides had broken into a foam of plant
bloom and bees, as sea waves break and bloom on a rock shore.

*The Mountains of California*

In reading John Muir's *Travels in Alaska* and *The Cruise of the
Corwin* and other works, one finds an abundance of commentary on Native American cultures. Yet no critic to date has devoted more
than several pages of interpretation of this commentary.[1] This study will
attempt a closer examination of John Muir's writings and notes on Indians
in order to reveal a clear relationship between his own environmental philosophy and that of primal cultures. The Indians of California and Alaska
not only confirmed Muir's belief in the need for a harmonious relationship

with nature but also inspired him to an even greater awareness of the intricacies of this relationship.

Early in his life on a farm in Wisconsin, after his immigration from Scotland in 1849, Muir recalls in *Boyhood and Youth* how nature's sermons were far more interesting to him than the churchy sermons of his stern Calvinistic father. God appeared to be so loving in the wilds of Wisconsin and so wrathful and condemning in the wilds of his father's soul. Daniel Muir, more than anyone else, was responsible for his son John's turning to nature for spiritual comfort. Muir's new god spoke to him in bird notes, in the rapids of the Hiwassee River, in the plants of the forest floor; his father's old god spoke with wrath and vengeance and reprisal for failing to listen to a message of overwhelming condemnation. How could God speak so gently in a lark's voice, in the invigorating voice of wind in the pines, if He was such a god of vengeance? Where is the vengeance in flower petal music, questioned the youthful Muir.

By the time young John Muir liberated himself from the clutches of his father's self-centered bigotry and studied at the University of Wisconsin and read Emerson and Thoreau, he was ripe for a thousand-mile walk, particularly after almost losing sight in one eye as a result of a factory accident in Indianapolis after his studies had been completed. Muir did follow some of the advice given in the Bible; he followed Solomon's lead of studying the ancient cedars and Christ's call to consider the lilies of the field. The deeper he traveled into the forests of the Deep South, the more familiar he became with a realistic wilderness which had malaria-ridden mosquitoes, alligators, and poisonous snakes. But each and every creature had just as much right to exist as man. *A Thousand-Mile Walk* is indeed a diatribe against a man-centered Calvinistic god and a defense of wildlife to remain forever free and wild. For too long has anthropocentric Western man claimed his natural superiority over all other living things with the Bible as his point d'appui. Muir, following Thoreau's example, defended wildlife by chastising tunnel-visioned humanity, and most of all the Daniel Muirs of this world, the epitome of tunnel vision.

A *Thousand-Mile Walk* is a polemic against his father's narrow philosophy which assumes God made the world for man first and God would reward hard work in the cultivation of fields and in the clearing of savage forests. Man should never let his attention wander from God through such devious pleasures as reading (other than His Bible), idle time and its idle occupations, and above all, enjoyment of the savage state of nature. Daniel Muir believed that nature must be redeemed and put to good use for the benefit of the most sacred creation in the cosmos, *man*. If one were foolish enough to write about untamed nature in the form of such a scandalous essay as "A Perilous Night on Shasta's Summit," he would probably suffer God's damnation and could only be saved by His most sacred grace. The only place where one can find God's thoughts, God's language, is in the Bible. To search for God anywhere else other than the Bible is to be a most grievous sinner.[2]

In 1867, two years after the close of the Civil War, Muir set forth on foot to walk from Indiana south to Florida in order to see God through botanizing and observing wildlife, something forbidden by his father a few years earlier. When he was sternly chastised by a southern farmer for not finding some constructive work to do, he retorted, whose advice should I follow, Christ's command to consider the lilies of the field, or yours? He easily won his argument. He lost himself in the beauty of the gaps and mountains of Tennessee. By the time he arrived in northern Florida, he came to view alligators as his friends and brothers:

> Many good people believe that alligators were created by the Devil, thus accounting for their all-consuming appetite and ugliness. But doubtless these creatures are happy and fill the place assigned them by the great Creator of us all. Fierce and cruel they appear to us, but beautiful in the eyes of God. They, also, are his children, for He hears their cries, cares for them tenderly, and provides their daily bread.[3]

As *all* men are brothers, Muir is suggesting that all creatures are brothers and equal in the eyes of their creator, an idea innately similar to that of the Native American.

A bit later in *A Thousand-Mile Walk*, Muir expresses his views on man's domination over the animal world even more strongly; one cannot help but think the following passage was addressed to his father:

> Let a Christian hunter go to the Lord's woods and kill his well-kept beasts, or wild Indians, and it is well; but let an enterprising specimen of these proper predestined victims go to houses and fields and kill the most worthless person of the vertical godlike killers,—oh! that is horribly unorthodox, and on the part of the Indians, atrocious murder! Well, I have precious little sympathy for the selfish propriety of civilized man, and if a war of races should occur between the wild beasts and Lord Man, I would be tempted to sympathize with the bears.[4]

Herman Melville's creature called Moby Dick may be an illustration of a similar sympathy for nature's dominance of man. Anticipating Aldo Leopold's *A Sand County Almanac* by over a half century, John Muir writes in his *A Thousand-Mile Walk*:

> Now, it seems to occur to these far-seeing teachers that Nature's object in making animals and plants might possibly be first of all the happiness of each one of them, not the creation of all for the happiness of one. Why should man value himself as more than a small part of the one great unit of creation? And what creature of all that the Lord has taken the pains to make is not essential to the completeness of that unit—the cosmos? The universe would be incomplete without man; but it would also be incomplete without the smallest trans-microscopic creature that dwells beyond our conceitful eyes and knowledge.[5]

Muir had to recover from transmicroscopic malaria (contracted in Florida) before he could travel on to the Sierra Nevada of California. In these sacred mountains he could examine God's creation with an unbiased mind and read hieroglyphic language to absorb as much metaphysical knowledge of the cosmos as possible. His experience of sheepherding in 1869, recorded in *My First Summer in the Sierra*, effuses with joy in the spiritual glow of landscapes with waterfall psalms and dew as manna for plants, crystals and flowers reflecting the Creator, and intense spiritual presence in crimson clouds of sunset and alpine glow. During this first summer, he learned to appreciate the Maidu Indians' sense of harmony with spiritual landscapes, as we shall see later in this study. The Indian and not Daniel Muir served as a better pathway to the Creator, as the Indian could read and interpret nature's hieroglyphic language. In the Sierra Nevada Muir notes that the Indian could make do with little while whites were "food poor." The Native American was able to translate his knowledge of nature into harmonious survival.

Hieroglyphic language, or "fossil poetry" as Emerson calls it, abounded from foothills to snowfields of the Sierra. Muir began to learn the *abc's* that first summer in 1869. As he notes early in the book, pines are definite symbols; they are "divine hieroglyphics written in sunbeams."[6] The landscapes themselves are divine pages of a spiritual manuscript transcribed in the form of river songs, stone sermons, and psalms of wildness. Since so many members of the human race have closed themselves to this ancient theism, Muir felt it to be his duty and responsibility to learn and decipher this neglected living scripture. He must listen to the many wild stories nature has to tell.

During the summer of 1869, Muir began to understand that nature is capable of restoring the human's sense of inner harmony which may be lost in mechanized society. The very notes of a wood thrush sift through the wilderness as the voice of God.[7] The sun energizes the human body to make it tingle,[8] and thunder vibrates with "electric spirituality."[9] In short, the sounds, sights, and feelings one receives in the wilderness of the Sierra and, as he will later discover, coastal Alaska or Mount Rainier, restore the

inner and outer body with wholeness which it somehow loses on the side-
walks of San Francisco or New York. As young John Muir slept out in the
mountains of California in 1869, he became cognizant of the physical and
psychological powers of plants. In this sense Muir intuitively recognized
certain mystical principles of Shamanism with which he would become
familiar in his excursions to Alaska ten years later.

He writes in *My First Summer in the Sierra*, "Only spread a fern
frond over a man's head and worldly cares are cast out and freedom and
beauty and peace come in."[10] Every chance he could, he slept under fern
fronds and stars because those fronds were "strangely impressive."[11] And
pine trees, "as every mountaineer knows," explains Muir, have a kind of
magic power.[12] In September 1874 Muir wrote to an old Madison friend,
Mrs. Ezra S. Carr, to explain that goldenrods "are hopeful and strength-
giving beyond any other flowers that I know."[13] It is no wonder that Muir,
like Black Elk and other American Indian medicine men, referred to plants
as people. Flowers, ferns, trees, and the mountains themselves realign the
human to mystical powers, flowing and pulsing about our planet, from
which civilization shields us by means of dead cinder block and steel gird-
ers. Forests, the wilderness in general, then, are of value to the human race
for a sacred manner of living.

John Muir also learned about balance and harmony from rugged
mountain slopes. Perched at an altitude of 12,800 feet on the treacherous
flanks of Mount Ritter one day in October 1872, Muir faced his doom. He
had inched his way up toward the summit to gain a broad view of the high
Sierra. He had picked his holds with intense caution, but he was brought to
a dead stop with nowhere to go. There were no more handholds! It appeared
to him that he *must* fall. In Muir's own words:

> When this final danger flashed upon me, I became nerve-shaken
> for the first time since setting foot on the mountains, and my
> mind seemed to fill with a stifling smoke. But this terrible eclipse
> lasted only a moment, when life blazed forth again with preter-
> natural clearness. I seemed suddenly to become possessed of a

new sense. The other self, bygone experiences, Instinct, or Guard-
ian Angel,—call it what you will,—came forward and assumed
control.[14]

Then his muscles became firm and his eyes perceived every "rift and flaw"
in the cliff above him. Soon he stood on the summit of Mount Ritter. Stephen Fox in *John Muir and His Legacy* believes the "other self" of Muir,
brought out so keenly by this awesome mountain slope, was a manifesta-
tion of his "psychic integration." Through this integration gained so peril-
ously, Muir was able to attune himself to the metaphysical forces of nature.

The closer the human being can become with the wilderness of our
planet and universe, the stronger his integration will become. "Civilized"
living tends to dull our receptivity, according to Muir. The American
Indians with whom Muir would come in contact aided immeasurably his
understanding of human integration with nature. By 1879 John Muir realized that the small populations of Tlingits and Yup'iks of Alaska, before
the coming of white man, were completely integrated with their natural
environment and lived in essential harmony and happiness for countless
generations. Because the Indian can sense "a spirit was embodied in every
mountain stream and waterfall," he has, Muir believed, a true reverence for
nature.[15] Civilization, on the other hand, wants to control nature and use it
for its own benefit, even if this means destroying an entire redwood forest
in the process. Muir writes in *Our National Parks* that pioneers, "claiming
Heaven as their guide, regarded God's trees as only a larger kind of perni-
cious weeds, extremely hard to get rid of."[16]

John Muir sincerely believed that we are capable of living in harmony with our Earth planet. Bee farming serves as a case in point of a
lucrative industry which does no harm to the environment. Arctic reindeer
herding as practiced by the Chukchi tribesmen of Siberia serves as another
illustration. We must attempt to accommodate ourselves to the local environment and understand its delicate balances in order to maintain the
*original* harmony. Clearly Muir gradually realized that early day primal
cultures possessed an intuitive understanding of natural harmonies, and

for this reason his Indian education in California and more importantly in Alaska was of profound significance.

## WISCONSIN AND CALIFORNIA

While John Muir had to overcome his boyhood fears of and prejudices against the Winnebago Indians of Wisconsin and later of the Indians of the Far West, he did come to appreciate Indians as his natural environmental mentors. They had adapted to North America over hundreds of generations and had much environmental wisdom to share with the white man. But because nineteenth-century Euro-Americans did little listening to cultures they were in the processing of subjugating, the settlers of Muir's day gained little or no land wisdom from their native brethren. Muir, as a youth, quite naturally was somewhat affected by prevailing attitudes toward Indians, and it wasn't until he had come to know individual Maidu, Tlingit, and Yup'ik natives that he was able to shed prejudice and learn from them. By the 1880s John Muir fully appreciated American Indian adaptivity to the land so strongly reflected in their lifestyle, language, social customs, mythology, and religion. Like Henry David Thoreau in Maine, Muir enhanced his understanding of Indian cultures by traveling, living, and working with them first in California and then in Alaska.

It must be pointed out that even as early as the 1850s, a youthful John Muir strongly sympathized with the downtrodden Indian and seriously questioned harsh attitudes toward Native Americans, but he first had to overcome some fearful experiences in Wisconsin which inevitably tainted his later concepts of Indians in general. Had he met with Mountain Wolf Woman of the Winnebago tribe (whose biography is recorded in the book *Mountain Wolf Woman*), surely his difficulties of overcoming prejudices would have been made easier. Nonetheless, after working with a Maidu Indian shepherd in 1869 and after several excursions to Alaska in the 1870s and 1880s where Muir lived among the various Tlingit tribes including Chilcats, Hoonas, and Takus, he grew to respect and honor their beliefs, customs, and wisdom. Their joyous adaptability to harsh surroundings gave Muir a clue that Native Americans had maintained a sound and harmonious pattern of living which was threatened by a supposedly more sophisticated civilization. But let us first go back in time to his boyhood.

When the Muir family moved from Scotland to Wisconsin in 1849, they soon became aware of weary and forlorn bands of Winnebago Indians who begged for food. After a short while, young Muir's favorite horse was stolen by one of those Indians, who treated the animal quite cruelly, as the Muirs later learned. They heard of valuable things being stolen from their neighbors' farms as well. At times the Winnebagos took it upon themselves to slaughter farmers' livestock for food. All of this naturally frightened the young lad from Scotland. Nonetheless, Muir listened with eager intentness to an argument between his stern father and a neighbor over Indian land rights which he later recalled in his autobiography, *The Story of My Boyhood and Youth*:

I well remember my father's discussing with a Scotch neighbor, a Mr. George Mair, the Indian question as to the rightful ownership of the soil. Mr. Mair remarked one day that it was pitiful to see how the unfortunate Indians, children of Nature living on the natural products of the soil, hunting, fishing, and even cultivating small cornfields on the most fertile spots, were now being robbed of their lands and pushed relentlessly back into narrower and narrower limits by alien races who were cutting off their means of livelihood. Father replied that surely it could have never been the intention of God to allow Indians to rove and hunt over so fertile a country and hold it forever in unproductive wildness, while Scotch and Irish and English farmers could put it to so much better use. Where an Indian required thousands of acres for his family, these acres in the hands of the industrious, God-fearing farmers would support ten or a hundred times more people in a far worthier manner, while at the same time helping to spread the gospel. Mr. Mair urged that such farming as our first immigrants

were practicing was in many ways rude and full of mistakes of
ignorance, yet, rude as it was, and ill-tilled as were most of our
Wisconsin farms by unskilled, inexperienced settlers who had
been merchants and mechanics and servants in the old countries, how should we like to have specially trained and educated
farmers drive us out of our homes and farms, such as they were,
making use of the same arguments, that God could never have
intended such ignorant, unprofitable, devastating farmers as we
were to occupy land upon which scientific farmers could raise five
or ten times as much on each acre as we did? And I well remember thinking that Mr. Mair had the better side of the argument. It
then seemed to me that, whatever the final outcome might be, it
was at this state of the fight only an example of the rule of might
with but little or no thought for the right or welfare of the other
fellow if he were the weaker; that "they should keep who can," as
Wordsworth makes the marauding Scottish Highlanders say.[17]

So, despite the fact that Muir recollected Winnebagoes as "blackmailing,"
"pig killing," "cruel," and "fearful," he did sympathize with their plight,
and such an early sympathy later helped inculcate a deeper appreciation
for Indian cultures with which he became more familiar. Such a positive attitude may have come about, in part at least, through his reaction
against his father's overly stern Calvinism. As Thomas J. Lyon points out,
"The chief aspect of Calvinism which Muir later rejected or outgrew was its
man-centeredness."[18] Euro-American culture was, for Muir, particularly
anthropocentric, especially in its biased attitudes toward seemingly alien
Indian cultures. As we shall see, Muir himself fell victim to anthropocen-
trism after he had settled in the mountains of California where he encountered Maidu Indians. But surely Muir's prejudices were short-lived once he
overcame what we call today "culture shock."

　　　Quite fortunately John Muir, at the age of twenty-two, left his father's
strict household where hard work was the rule and playing and storytelling
were the exceptions. As a special student at the University of Wisconsin,

he was able to take whichever courses had the most intellectual appeal. In Madison he studied under Professor Ezra Slocum Carr, who, along with his Mrs. Jeanne Carr, introduced Muir to the writings of Ralph Waldo Emerson and Henry David Thoreau. In addition to Emerson's essay "Nature," probably Thoreau's essays on Maine had the most appeal to Muir because of the New England author's philosophical descriptions of nature and more specifically Thoreau's growing appreciation of culturally subjugated American Indians who managed to maintain some of their ancient ways. As will be shown, in many respects Muir's *Travels in Alaska* (1916) and Thoreau's *Maine Woods* (1864) are comparable works insofar as they both record the impact of American Indian cultures on the minds of the authors.

When Muir arrived in California in 1868 after his thousand-mile walk from Indiana to Florida, he chose to work as a shepherd during the summer and early fall in the foothills and high country of the Sierra. The journal he kept became the basis of *My First Summer in the Sierra* (1911). He worked for Mr. Delaney, an ex-seminarian from Manooth, Ireland, who was sensitive to young Muir's quest for the wild, allowing him to take numerous rambles into those shining mountains. His working companions were Billy, Carlo (a sheepdog), a "Chinaman," and a Maidu Indian. This Maidu Indian (who remains nameless in the book) was to become Muir's first real contact with Indian culture since his fearful days in Wisconsin with the Winnebago Indians. While his impressions of Indians in general remain ambivalent at this stage of his life, Muir's shy respect and admiration for his Maidu Indian coworker are clearly seen in *My First Summer in the Sierra*.

Generally speaking, we can see that Muir's comments on collective Indian cultures of California are at best ambivalent, while his reaction to his Maidu Indian companion is quite positive. Such a pattern of racial acceptance is quite normal as we grow to appreciate another race through individuals first. But first let us briefly examine his ambivalent commentary on Indian cultures in general. Muir could not understand why Maidu Indians were exceptionally unclean in body, especially since they lived in the pure and fresh wilderness. It seemed somewhat strange for

MAIDU INDIANS OF CALIFORNIA BURNING THEIR DEAD.

a Scotsman that these people left no traces of their civilization.[19] As of 1869 Muir apparently did not consider their legends of any lasting importance (if indeed he was aware of them) as did many readers of San Francisco's earliest newspapers. Many of his terms of description of this Indian tribe were clearly negative: "dirty," "garrulous as jays," "superstitious," "deadly," "lazy," "squirrelish," and "wife stealing." They begged for food and whiskey (later Muir would learn that Western civilization had something to do with this).

On the other hand, he expressed sympathy with the reaction of Chief Tenaya to his expulsion from Yosemite.[20] In the later writings incorporated in *The Mountains of California* Muir quotes Chief Tenaya's sad but powerful speech occasioned by his expulsion. In this speech Chief Tenaya warns that their spirits will come to haunt the white man. Writing to Mrs. Carr in the autumn of 1871, Muir poetically confirms Chief Tenaya's prophecy by stating that "I wish you could see Lake Tenaya. It is one of the most perfectly and richly spiritual places in the mountains, and I would like to preempt there."[21] Muir believed that the Indians of the Shasta region were, like Chief Tenaya, "inexorably demoralized."[22]

As Muir was beginning to realize, when the Indian was allowed to remain on his land, he was able to maintain a sense of harmony as evidenced by the joyous pine nut feasts in the Sierra forests.[23] In these forests the Indian tribes made full use of all edible resources (as did Thoreau's Penobscot Indians in the Maine woods) including fruits and berries such as the manzanita (the juice of which was made into a wild cider), sequoia juice, and even such insects as grasshoppers and ants.[24] Muir noted, additionally, that mountain and canyon tribes possessed the virtues of endurance, intelligence, and tireless patience while hunting wild animals of the region.[25]

And certainly the young Scotsman admired the mountain tribes' respect for the dead.[26] Muir describes the death wailing of Indians in the high Sierra:

The fire glare and the wild wailing came with indescribable impressiveness through the still dark woods. I listened eagerly as the weird curves of woe swelled and cadenced, now rising steep like glacial precipices, now swooping low in polished slopes. Falling boulders and rushing streams and wind tones caught from rock and tree were in it.[27]

Their death song seemed to reflect the very spirit of the landscape. So while there are many negative reactions to the Indians of California, there are also a significant number of positive reactions in Muir's early writings.

Clearly Edwin Way Teale, in *The Wilderness World of John Muir*, could have readily found further evidence than he did for Muir's admiration of the California Indian's "manner . . . [of adapting] themselves to their surroundings [which] fitted in with nature's ways, leaving hardly a scar on the landscape."[28] Muir's ambivalent attitude toward California Indians can be seen in the following significant statement from *My First Summer in the*

*Sierra*: "Perhaps if I knew them better, I should like them better. The worst thing about them is their uncleanliness."[29]

However, the *one* Indian Muir did get to know better during his first summer in the Sierra was the Maidu Indian sheepherder. This Indian always kept in the background and never asserted himself. He was an extremely silent walker in the woods,[30] a patient hunter, and he seemed incapable of damaging the landscape as opposed to the noisy, assertive white man. He was self-sufficient in the wilderness and not "food poor" as were his white coworkers.[31] It seems likely Muir watched this Indian gather and prepare foods for he writes, "Like the Indians, we ought to know how to get the starch out of fern and saxifrage stalks, lily bulbs, pine bark etc. Our education unlike the Indian's has been sadly neglected for many generations. Wild rice would be good."[32] If only the white man could be truly educated. The Indian did not have to be taught Thoreau's principle of simplicity. Making do with little epitomized this individual Maidu Indian's lifestyle. On the evening of July 8, Muir came to realize the natural superiority of a Maidu Indian in his own territory of the mountains of California:

> The Indian lay down away from the fire last night, without blankets, having nothing on, by way of clothing, but a pair of blue overalls and a calico shirt wet with sweat. The night air is chilly at this elevation, and we gave him some horse-blankets, but he didn't seem to care for them. A fine thing to be independent of clothing where it is so hard to carry. When food is scarce, he can live on whatever comes in his way—a few being roots, bird eggs, grasshoppers, black ants, fat wasp or bumblebee larvae, without feeling that he is doing anything worth mention, so I have been told.[33]

Here, then is an exemplar of Emersonian self-reliance and Thoreauvian simplicity. Whether or not this Indian inspired Muir's deeper appreciation for mountains, sometimes expressed in Shelleyian "bursts of ecstasy," is a matter of conjecture, but I am inclined to think that there was, at least, an indirect influence.[34] It is interesting to note that in numerous places in

*My First Summer in the Sierra* and later in *The Mountains of California* he refers to creatures as people, for example, insect people and bird people. Certainly the Indian influenced Muir's own manner of going into the wild country with no heavy burdens. Tea and breadcrumbs sustained Muir for days on end.

Muir's attitudes toward Indians suffered somewhat of a setback in 1878 when he joined a US Coast and Geodetic Survey to go to the wild country of the Nevada-Utah border, country of the enemy of the Maidu Indians, the Paiutes. This was the year of Indian unrest and wars in Idaho to the north of the survey party. Quite naturally, Muir's old Wisconsin fears of Indians surfaced strongly. He wrote to his future bride's mother, Mrs. Strentzel, that

> If an explorer of God's fine wilderness should wait until every danger be removed, then he would wait until the sun set. The war country lies to the north of our line of work, some two or three hundred miles. Some of the Pah Utes [sic] have gone north to join the Bannocks, and those left behind are not to be trusted, but we shall be well armed, and they will not dare to attack a party like ours unless they mean to declare war, however gladly they might seize the opportunity of killing a lonely and unknown explorer. In any case we will never be more than two hundred miles from the railroad.[35]

## TRAVELS IN PANHANDLE ALASKA

Thirty years after John Muir first immigrated to America, and ten years after his arrival in the Sierra Nevada, he set sail in May 1879 aboard the *Dakota* for the virgin wilderness of Alaska. His main object was to study the immense living glaciers of "cup handle" Alaska. Here, between May and November, he would confirm his suspicions that our planet's landscape is constantly evolving and changing because of slow and powerful natural forces. But he, too, would evolve and change from his somewhat ambivalent stance toward various Indian cultures to one of positive admiration after he overcame culture shock.

It is interesting to note that the famous Swiss anthropologist and contemporary of John Muir, Adolph Bandelier (1840–1914), while deeply fascinated with Indian cultures of the Southwest, remained in his writings as late as 1890 extremely judgmental. In his *Delight Makers*, a novel of prehistoric Pueblo Indians written at age fifty, Bandelier, as narrator, injects invidious invectives about Indians being sedentary, unprofitable workers having no curiosity about nature and speaking childlike languages.

John Muir may have shared some of these views earlier in life, but in Alaska he liberated himself from them. Two more trips to Alaska in 1880 and 1890 form the fabric of *Travels in Alaska*, first published one year after his death and compiled from his journal and previously published magazine articles. His trip from May to September of 1881 became the basis of *The Cruise of the Corwin*, and a fifth trip between May and July 1899 under the title "Cruising with the Harriman—Alaska Expedition," was finally published in *John of the Mountains* edited by Linnie Marsh Wolfe in 1938.

On his first Alaskan trip, Muir met Samuel H. Young, a missionary at Fort Wrangell, and the two became traveling companions throughout the panhandle, where Muir would study glaciers and Young would preach to the Indians. Both men were Thoreau and Emerson enthusiasts, and both had copies of the New Englanders' works. My best guess is that Muir carried with him an 1864 edition of Thoreau's *Maine Woods*. If he did not physically have that book he certainly did mentally, for there are many striking philosophical similarities in their growing fascination for Native American cultures. Both books are based on three separate excursions to the wilderness, and both Thoreau and Muir experience culture shock when they first enter Indian worlds. But the two writers begin to respect and admire the Indian once they mingle with and make friends with the people. They both attempt to learn the native dialects as well as mythology and Indian lifestyles. Whether or not Muir consciously modeled *Travels in Alaska* (compiled on his deathbed) on *The Maine Woods* (compiled after

Thoreau's death) is a moot point. But permit me to digress a while with a brief comparison of Thoreau's and Muir's Indian education.

Thoreau's first excursion into Maine in 1846 (while he is still residing at Walden Pond) provides him with his first substantial contact with Indian culture. At first he is shocked by the "shabby," "woe begone," "dull," "greasy-looking," "sluggish," "sinister," and "slouching" looks of the Penobscot Indians in general and Louis Neptune in particular. He would have been happier to see a man tortured at the stake by wild Indians than to see these frightfully demoralized ignoble savages who had little interest in nature and seemed to comprise the lower part of the white man's world.

Likewise Muir begins *Travels in Alaska* by describing coastal Indians with "hideous face paint," and "fearful" and "superstitious" manners. He was amazed that Tlingits were not as curious about the wild, beautiful country as he. But both Thoreau and Muir overcome their hesitancy to accept another culture through their contact with individual Indians, Muir on his first excursion and Thoreau on his second and third excursions. Perhaps Muir's acquaintance with the Maidu Indian shepherd ten years earlier enabled him to overcome his shock and disdain for certain customs and habits of the Tlingits more quickly than Thoreau was able to overcome his difficulties with the Penobscots. Most of Thoreau's knowledge of Indians as of 1846 was book knowledge, not personal acquaintance. However, Thoreau did come to appreciate the Indian as his teacher and metaphysical guide. In 1853, Thoreau met Joe Aitteon, his first nonwhite wilderness guide. Through Aitteon, Thoreau gained an intense interest in the Penobscot language and Penobscot wilderness living. Describing his evening campfire education, Thoreau writes:

While lying there listening to the Indians, I amused myself by trying to guess at their subject by their gestures, or some proper name introduced. There can be no more startling evidence of their being distinct and comparatively aboriginal race, than to hear this unaltered Indian language, which white man cannot speak nor understand. We may suspect change and deterioration in almost

every other particular but the language which is so wholly unin-
telligible to us. It took me by surprise, though I had found so many
arrow-heads and convinced me that the Indian was not the inven-
tion of historians and poets . . . these Abenakis gossiped, laughed,
and jested, in the language which has been spoken in New England who shall say how long? These were the sounds that issued
from the wigwams of this country before Columbus was born;
they have not yet died away; and, with remarkably few exceptions,
the language of their forefathers is still copious enough for them.
I felt that I stood, or rather lay, as near to the primitive man of
America, that night, as any of its discoverers ever did.[36]

This Indian language was close to nature—so close Thoreau conjectures
in his *Indian Notebooks* that the Indian looks about him in nature to find
some natural object to aid his expression.[37] Penobscot language brought
Thoreau to the very ground as its sounds were the sounds of nature unfil-
tered and undigested by civilized man. Though this language was at first
totally incomprehensible, Thoreau did make the effort to learn it at an
elementary level as Muir would learn Alaskan tongues. Both Thoreau and
Muir could see the direct natural sense of Indian languages. For example,
Thoreau asked what the word *Sebamook* meant:

Tahmunt said, "Ugh! I know," and he rose up partly on the moose-
hide—"like here is a place, and there is a place," pointing to the
different parts of the hide, "and you take water from there and
fill this, and it stays here; that is Sebamook." I understood him to
mean that it was a reservoir of water which did not run away, the
river coming in on one side and passing out again near the same
place, leaving a permanent bay.[38]

*Sebamook*, then, is a word full of the forces of nature uttered in three
syllables. Therein lies a good bit of metaphysical significance for Thoreau.
Many pages of the second essay "Chesuncook" of *The Maine Woods* are

taken up with a discussion of Indian vocabulary predominantly relating to natural phenomena (e.g., Penobscot River meaning originally the name of a section of the main channel, from the head of the tidewater to a short distance above Oldtown). Every word is steeped in nature; this is important to a nineteenth-century philosopher whose every thought is steeped in nature.

Likewise the Indian living patterns are rooted in nature as were Thoreau's at Walden Pond and Muir's in the Sierra. Thoreau writes, "I narrowly watched his motions, and listened attentively to his observations, for we had employed an Indian mainly that I might have an opportunity to study his ways" (P. 95). Joe Aitteon's native ingenuity exemplified for Thoreau an ideal blend of man in nature. From the bark of a birch tree, for instance, he made a hunting horn and a torch to keep insects away at nighttime. The white lumberman and other backwoodsmen learned much from the Indian in this regard. Like Muir with the Maidu Indians, Thoreau marveled at Joe's manner of silent walking during a moose hunt: ". . . he stepped lightly and gracefully, stealing through the bushes with the least possible noise, in a way in which no white man does, as it were, finding a place for his foot each time" (P. 112). No one can deny the importance of Thoreau's education at Harvard, yet the Penobscots of Maine were surely of equal significance in the development of Thoreau the philosopher.

Thoreau's third excursion to Maine in 1857, ten years after his Walden experiment and three years after the publication of *Walden*, provided him a continuing Indian education through a second native guide, Joe Polis. Thoreau agreed to teach Polis all he knew if Polis would teach him all he knew. Aitteon and Polis were for Thoreau what Kadachan and Toyatte would be for Muir, as we shall see. Thoreau drilled Polis with questions on the Penobscot language. He learned that there is as direct a connection between language and natural phenomena as there is between mythology and natural phenomena. For instance " 'apmoozenegamook' means a lake that is crossed because the usual course lies across it not along it" (P. 238). He observed that the Penobscot language "was wild and refreshing sound, like that of the wind among the pines, or the booming of the surf on the shore" (P. 169). When Joe Polis sang aloud in his own tongue by a campfire at night, Thoreau remarked that "his singing carried me back to the period of the discovery of America, to San Salvador and the Incas, when Europeans first encountered the simple faith of the Indian" (P. 179).

And, as with Aitteon, Polis taught Thoreau much about the Indian's natural ingenuity. Certain species of plants could be used for medicinal purposes. The inner bark of the aspen, for instance, was good for sore eyes (P. 309). Lily bulbs made an excellent wild soup, and black spruce roots, when split, made good threads for repairing leaky canoes with a tree bark patch. Certain oils made from tree barks served as good insect repellent. The Indian always seemed to know where he was in the woods or on a misty lake. He had an uncanny sense of direction, as Thoreau notes:

> I could only occasionally perceive his trail in the moss, and yet he did not appear to look down nor hesitated an instant, but led us out exactly to his canoe. This surprised me, for without a compass, or the sight or noise of the river to guide us, we could have retraced our steps but a short distance, with a great deal of pains and very slowly, using a laborious circumspection. But it was evident that he could go back through the forest wherever he had been during the day. (P. 251)

All of this proved to Thoreau that men living close to nature will have nature deeply embedded in their spirits, language, and lifestyle. Of course, not all was rosy; Thoreau did have reservations about Polis's seemingly ruthless moose hunting tactics and his apparent lack of concern for Thoreau's companion who had been lost one night.

But through the Indian's closeness to nature came his mythological fabrications which fascinated the visitor from Concord. The Indian poet of nature invented, in ancient times, a mythological moose out of the land:

> While we were crossing this bay, where Mount Kineo rose dark before us, within two or three miles, the Indian repeated the

tradition respecting this mountain's having anciently been a cow moose,—how a mighty Indian hunter, whose name I forget, succeeding in killing this queen of the moose tribe with great difficulty, while her calf was killed somewhere among the islands of Penobscot Bay, and, to his eyes, this mountain had still the form of the moose in a reclining posture, its precipitous side presenting the outline of her head. (P. 172)

Perhaps it was no small coincidence for Thoreau that Mount Kineo, so he was told, was a good source of hornstone, used for making arrowheads and hatchets (P. 176). Through the Indian's knowledge of and feeling for nature, then, Thoreau gained a deeper appreciation for intangible qualities of the wilderness. He himself became Indianized somewhat in his perceptions of Maine, far more so in 1857 than during his first excursion to Maine in 1846. As we shall see, a similar Indianization process occurs for John Muir in Alaska.

Thoreau writes in this last *Maine Woods* essay, "Allegash and East Branch," that "Nature must have made a thousand revelations to them which are still secrets to us" (P. 181). Thoreau began to learn some of these secrets; nowhere better can this be seen than in the 1857 excursion. Through the Indian Thoreau gained a multidimensional appreciation and psychic integration of the wilds which he did not have on his first trip. Referring to the "will-o'-the-wisp" light coming from phosphorescent deadwood, he explains that a white man's scientific explanation of the phenomenon is of little interest to him:

I let science slide, and rejoiced in that light as if it had been a fellow-creature. I saw that it was excellent, and was very glad to know that it was so cheap. A scientific *explanation*, as it is called, would have been altogether out of place there . . . Your so-called wise man goes trying to persuade himself that there is no entity there but himself . . . but it is a great deal easier to believe the truth. It suggested, too, that the same experience always gives birth to the same sort of belief or religion. One revelation has been made

to the Indian, another to the white man. I have much to learn of
the Indian, nothing of the missionary. I am not sure but all that
would tempt me to teach the Indian my religion would be his
promise to teach me his. Long enough I had heard of irrelevant
things; now at length I was glad to make acquaintance with the
light that dwells in the rotten wood. Where is all your knowledge
gone to? It evaporates completely, for it has no depth. (Pp. 181–82)

It is the metaphysical speculation, epistemology, which attracts Thoreau,
not the rote science of white civilization or the Sunday school religion of
the churches of Concord. The Indian has given him an epistemological
pathway through the wood. In this sense Polis is like Virgil leading Dante
toward a deeper knowledge of nature and away from the idée fixe of the
white man. Thoreau must learn the language of nature through the Indian.
Joe Polis spoke such a language when he talked to a muskrat:

And sitting flat on the bank, he began to make a curious squeak-
ing, wiry sound with his lips, exerting himself considerably. I was
greatly surprised,—thought that I had at last got into the wilderness, and that he was a wild man indeed, to be talking to a musquash! I did not know which of the two was the strangest to me.
He seemed suddenly to have quite forsaken humanity, and gone
over the musquash side. (Pp. 206–7)

Thoreau imitates Polis by talking in his own language to a spruce hawk:
"Such an impertinent fellow would occasionally try to alarm the world
about me. 'O,' said I, 'I am well acquainted with your family, I know your
cousins in Concord very well. Guess the mail's irregular in these parts,
and you'd like to hear from 'em' " (Pp. 218–19). And commenting on the
call of the wild loon, Thoreau writes, "I have heard a sound exactly like
it when breathing heavily through my own nostrils, half awake at ten at
night, suggesting my affinity to the loon; as if its language were but a dia-
lect of my own, after all" (P. 225). He, numerous times, repeats the sound

of the white-throated sparrow's "ah te ee te ee te," saying, "what a glorious time they must have in that wilderness, far from mankind and election day!" (P. 193). In other words Thoreau was capable of sensing through bird notes corresponding feelings for nature in his own soul. Indianized Thoreau writes, "My imagination personified the slopes themselves, as if by their very length they would waylay you and compel you to camp again on them before night. Some invisible glutton would seem to drop from the trees and gnaw at the heart of the solitary hunter who threaded those woods; and yet was I tempted to walk there" (P. 184). Clearly the Indian led Thoreau through the wilderness to metaphysical heights. It is no wonder that Muir's copy of *The Maine Woods* is heavily marked with underscorings.

Let us turn to Muir's Indian education in Panhandle Alaska as recorded in *Travels in Alaska*. Soon after Muir first arrived at Fort Wrangell, he was warned by white residents that he should beware of Indians on his glacial explorations, for they were a bad lot. Perhaps he relied upon his older feelings toward Winnebagos and Paiutes when he built a fire in the rainy woods to cause a weird glow in the sky which frightened the superstitious Indians of the area. Sounding somewhat like Hank Morgan in Mark Twain's *Connecticut Yankee in King Arthur's Court*, Muir takes pride in his seeming power over the local primitives by delighting in their wild fear. A few days later, when he discovered that the Indians at Wrangell wore "ridiculous" face paint, he assumed all the more the aspect of a superior lord slumming it.

While still at Wrangell Island, Muir was invited to a dance in which "excellent imitations were given the gait, gestures, and behaviors of several animals under different circumstances—walking, hunting, capturing, and devouring their prey, etc." And the animal movements "were so accurately imitated that they seemed the real thing."[39] Muir thought it was altogether a wonderful show, but he still remained somewhat aloof from these picturesque Indians until he began to observe their skillful use of the canoe and their joyous gathering of wild berries. When Muir sailed south to explore the ruins of a Stickeen village, he was altogether delighted:

The magnitude of the ruins and excellence of the workmanship manifest in them was about forty feet square, with walls built of planks two feet wide and six inches thick. The ridge pole of yellow cypress was two feet in diameter, forty feet long, and as round and true as if it had had been turned in a lathe; and though lying in the damp weeds it was perfectly sound . . . Each of the wall planks had evidently been hewn out of a whole log, and must have required steady deliberation as well as skill. This geometrical truthfulness was admirable; with the same tools not one in a thousand of our skilled mechanics could do as good work. Compared with it the bravest work of civilized backwoodsmen is feeble and bungling. The completeness of form, finish, and proportion of timbers suggested skill of a wild and positive kind, like that which guides the wood-pecker in drilling round holes, and the bee in making its cells.[40]

We can see here that this appreciation of the Indian imagination has increased markedly over his initially ambivalent reactions to the Maidu Indians of Yosemite.

Muir was captivated by Stickeen totem poles, so much so that he sketched them in his journal and described them with enthusiasm:

Some of the most imposing were said to commemorate some event of an historical character. But a telling display of family pride seemed to have been the prevailing motive. All the figures were more or less rude, and some were broadly grotesque, but there was never any feebleness of obscurity in the expression. On the contrary every feature showed grave force and decision; while the childish audacity displayed in the design, combined with manly strength in their execution, was truly wonderful.[41]

When a white missionary started chopping down one of these wonderful old totem poles for some private museum, Muir's sympathies were quickly aroused by the words of his newly found Tlingit friend, Kadachan, "How

THE SITE OF THE VILLAGE [STICKEEN] IS MARKED MOST INTER-
ESTINGLY BY CARVED TOTEM PILLARS, NOW MOSS-GROWN,
AND SOME OF THEM PICTURESQUELY PLANTED WITH TUFTS OF
GRASSES AND BUSHES. ONE CARVED POST IS SURMOUNTED BY A
BEAR, LIFE SIZE." JOHN MUIR, *JOHN OF THE MOUNTAINS.*]

would you like to have an Indian go to a graveyard and break down and
carry away a monument belonging to your family."[42] Perhaps Muir thought
that the warning given him by whites upon his arrival at Wrangell Island
of Indians being a "bad lot" should have been reversed!

Through the importance of the religious art of totem poles, then, Muir was first able to see the depths of humanity of Tlingit Indians. His first Indian traveling companion and guide, Chief Kadachan (somewhat like Thoreau's guide Joe Aitteon), was a happy and merry fellow who liked to tell stories and tales of his people and who could laugh at himself for failing to retrieve ducks he had shot. Kadachan's mother, on the other hand, had a woeful and sorrowful face like those of the Kwakuitl Indians of British Columbia described in Margaret Craven's moving novel, *I Heard the Owl Call My Name* (1973). Seeing Indian joy and sorrow helped Muir culturally adjust to Tlingits much like Margaret Craven's protagonist, Mark Brian. Muir began to laugh with Kadachan and to listen with care to his fascinating theories and stories about Alaskan wildlife in the midst of the superb icy fjords. Like Thoreau, Muir listened to stories and traditions by evening campfires: "After supper we sat long around our fire, listening to the Indians' stories about the wild animals, their hunting adventures, wars, traditions, religion and customs."[43] The California naturalist marveled at Indian explanations of animal behavior as in the following theory of why birds honk: "The Indians said that geese, swans, cranes, etc., making their long journeys in regular order thus called aloud to encourage each other and enabled them to keep stroke and time like men in rowing or marching (a sort of 'row, brothers, row' or 'Hip, hip' of marching soldiers.)"[44]

Muir began to sense that Indian interest in animal behavior was not only knowledgeable but insightful. He writes:

I greatly enjoyed the Indians' campfire talk this evening on their ancient customs, how they were taught by their parents when the whites came among them, their religion, ideas connected with the next world, the stars, plants, the behavior and language of animals under different circumstance, manner of getting a living, etc. When our talk was interrupted by the howling of a wolf on the opposite side of the strait, Kadachan puzzled the minister with the question, 'Have wolves souls?' The Indians believed that they have; giving a foundation of their belief that they are wise creatures who know how to catch seals and salmon by swimming slyly upon them with their heads hidden in a mouthful of grass, hunt deer in company, and always bring forth their young at the same and most favorable time of the year. I inquired how it was that with enemies so wise and powerful the deer were not all killed. Kadachan replied that wolves knew better than to kill them all and thus cut off their most important food-supply.[45]

Here is a strong evidence for the Tlingit's ecological understanding of his environment acquired through long years of observation. Indians had learned much from their land, and this is significant for Muir the natural philosopher. During the second excursion to Alaska in 1880 Muir gained further understanding of the Indians' relatedness to wildlife when he heard them address salmon as though they were humans, just like Jim Wallace in Margaret Craven's novel doing the same or Joe Polis addressing the muskrat in the Maine Woods. At the mouth of an Alaskan salmon stream Muir writes, "our Indians shouted joyfully, 'Hi yu salmon! Hi yu muck-a-muck!' "[46] John Muir had learned to address animals quite well back in Yosemite, particularly the Douglas squirrel as shown in *The Mountains of California* (1894). It is also wonderful, for Muir, that the Indians of Alaska conceive of heaven being populated with animals as well as humans.[47] As early as his boyhood years, Muir innately believed in the spirituality of animals,[48] and to see such a belief confirmed among these people in such an overwhelmingly beautiful panhandle Alaska with its icy fjords must have been a spiritual revelation for John Muir at age forty.

A spiritual bond between humans and animals necessitates our greater concern for and awareness of our *total* environment.

John Muir was equally fascinated by the rich legends and folktales of the Tlingits inspired by nature, some of which were recorded in *Travels in Alaska*, indicating he was not loath to record supernatural legends as Herbert Smith contends.[49] Smith makes this contention because Muir left out a tradition which is included in Young's book *Alaska Days with*

*John Muir* but not in *Travels in Alaska*. From the later published *John of the Mountains* it goes as follows:

> When a Stickeen Indian dies, the body is burned with feasting and chanting and bestowal of gifts. If these rites are properly celebrated, the soul on reaching the bank of a great river is ferried over, given a body, and guided through the woods far inland to a fruitful, gameful country and is happy. But in the case the death rites be imperfectly administered he is unable to get over the river and is compelled to wander, an unhappy ghost, in a wet, dark wood, and work mischief to the living. . . .[50]

It was more probably an oversight on Muir's part that he did not include this legend in *Travels in Alaska* considering how very late in his life he composed the book. But he did record an equally supernatural story in the book which here follows. It involves a sick Indian boy being examined by a Tlingit shaman who explains

> that the boy has lost his soul, and this is the way it happened. He was playing among the stones down on the beach when he saw a crawfish in the water, and made fun of it, pointing his finger at it saying, "oh, you crooked legs! Oh, you crooked legs! You can't walk straight; you go sidewise," which made the crab so angry that he reached out his long nippers, seized the lad's soul, pulled it out of him and made off with it into deep water. "And," continued the medicine-man, "unless his stolen soul is restored to him and put back in its place he will die. Your boy is really dead already; it is only his lonely, empty body that is living now, though it may continue to live in this way for a year or two, the boy will never be of any account, not strong, nor wise, nor brave."[51]

This story implies the need for a respectful relationship between humans and all creatures. Muir repeats yet another Indian tale heard on this 1880

trip concerning a legendary stout creature called Yek who was responsible for rain by whirling himself over the ocean to gather rain clouds.[52]
His interest in native mythologies continued to grow during the late 1880s
when he began composing *The Mountains of California* and *The Cruise of
the Corwin* (to be examined shortly), which contain further references to
Indian myths so steeped in nature.

In the opening of *The Mountains of California*, we find a reference
to the volcanic legends of the Pitt River Indians. "They tell of a fearful time
of darkness when the sky was black with ashes and smoke that threatened
every living thing with death, and that when at length the sun appeared
once more it was red like blood."[53] And again in the posthumously published *Steep Trails* (originally the Oregon and Washington essays were
in *Picturesque California*), Muir refers to the Indian legend of Mount
St. Helens and Mount Hood: "According to an Indian tradition, the river of
the Cascades once flowed through the basalt beneath a natural bridge that
was broken down during a mountain war, when the old volcanoes, Hood and
St. Helens, on opposite sides of the river, hurled rocks at each other, thus
forming a dam."[54] In *The Cruise of the Corwin* Muir writes, "This old volcano
[a prominent cone near St. Michael, Alaska] is said by the medicine men to
be the entrance to the spirit world for their tribe, and the rumbling sounds
heard occasionally are supposed to be caused by the spirits when they are
conducting in a dead Indian."[55] Like Henry Thoreau, John Muir intuitively
realized that nature is an important basis of mythology. And both Thoreau
and Muir precede Paul Ehrenreich, the twentieth-century German folklorist, in assuming that similar natural phenomena produce similar myths.[56]
Volcanoes, earthquakes, floods, etc., produce a rich variety of myths; but all
have the essential quality of eliciting a sense of awe at the forces of nature,
the forces of destruction and construction, and the fusion of spiritual and
material worlds, which Muir's concept of harmony clearly reflects. Indian
mythmaking, then, was for Muir yet another example of the Indian's harmonious and spiritual absorption of nature into his life and psyche.

Returning to *Travels in Alaska*, in addition to Tlingit art and
mythology, Indian society also enticed Muir. He commented on their great

respect for children: "Indeed, in all my travels I never saw a child, old or young, receive a blow or even a harsh word."[57] And a little later he writes, "I have never seen a child ill-used, even to the extent of an angry word. Scolding, so common a curse in civilization, is not known here at all. On the contrary the young are fondly indulged without being spoiled. Crying is very rarely heard."[58] Such observations are in marked contrast to the stern wrath of Muir's own father back in Scotland and Wisconsin. The joy of a live-and-let-live attitude was refreshing to Muir because he had experienced little of it as a boy. While Muir's father always stifled his son's curiosity, the Indian's "childlike attention was refreshing to see as compared with the deathlike apathy of weary town-dwellers, in whom natural curiosity has been quenched in toil and care and poor shallow comfort."[59]

Muir's own curiosity about the Indian way steadily increased the longer he stayed in Alaska. Like Thoreau, he attempted to learn some of the Indian tongue and in many instances recorded Indian words in his writings completely replacing English equivalents. Both *Travels in Alaska* and *The Maine Woods* have glossaries of Indian vocabulary. I list a few expressions from the main text of *Travels in Alaska*: *Hyas klosh* (good), *Hoon* (North Wind), *hi yu poojh* (much shooting), *sagh-a-ya* (are you sleeping well?), *Shookum chuck, shookum chuck!* (strong water, strong water!), *Friday, Tucktay* (shoreward, seaward), and the mixed English-Tlingit *hiyu kumtux hide* (glaciers know how to hide extremely well). Toward the end of his third excursion (July 1890) Muir began to speak a little Chinook: "I tried my Chinook and made out to say that I wanted to hire two of them in a few days to go a little back on the glacier and around the bay. They are seal-hunters and promised to come again with 'Charley,' who 'hi yu kumtux wawa Boston'—knew well how to speak English."[60] Muir began to comprehend that this northern language, rich in the physical aspects of a glaciated land, was the appropriate language to speak. Through the language one could better understand the environment, for environment was reflected so aptly in the language. Muir was in philosophical accord with Thoreau's conviction that the Indian "looks around him in the woods . . . to aid his expression."[61] With increasing pleasure Muir listened to and spoke the natural *wawa* of these Native Americans. After his Alaskan excursions, Muir did take note of California Indian tongues and respected their earthy appropriateness. For instance, in his chapter on the Douglas squirrel in *The Mountains of California*, Muir comments, "A King's River Indian told me that they call him 'Pillilloocet,' which, rapidly pronounced with the first syllable heavily accented, is not unlike the lusty exclamation he utters on his way up a tree when excited."[62] And Muir is appreciative of the Indian term for the Sierra Nevada—*Pyweek*—which means Shining Rock Mountains, exactly what Muir thought they should have been called in the first place.[63]

Of far more importance than his interest in art, mythology, and language is Muir's growing awareness of Indian wisdom and of the realization that all men are brothers. As earlier mentioned, Muir met the Reverend Samuel H. Young, a Presbyterian missionary at Fort Wrangell. When Young learned that Muir wished to visit coastal glaciers, he decided to go along to carry out his missionary work and enjoy some of Muir's philosophical insights. While on a canoe voyage northward during the trip of 1879, some Kake Indians visited Muir and Young's camp. Mr. Young asked the Indians if they would be interested in having a missionary, and Muir quotes the head of the family's reply: "We have not much to say to you fellows. We always do to Boston men as we have done to you, give a little of whatever we have, treat everybody well and never quarrel. This is all we have to say."[64] Muir lets the reader draw his own conclusions by adding no commentary of his own, though one can almost imagine the twinkle in his eye. The Scotsman of the Sierra, like Mark Brian of *I Heard the Owl Call My Name*, soon realizes that these coastal Indians are inherently more Christian than Christians, in that they fully understand Christ's teaching of atonement (or making up for one's sins) and charity because they practiced such virtues long before they ever heard of Christ. As Muir writes, "The Thlinkit [Tlingit] tribes give a hearty welcome to Christian missionaries. In particular they are quick to accept the doctrine of the atonement, because they themselves practice it, although to many of the civilized whites it is a stumbling block and rock of offense."[65] That the Indian should deprecate his inner moral nature by expressing a desire to learn from the missionary was for Muir ironic.

John Muir's good Indian friend Toyatte (of the 1879 voyage) made the supreme sacrifice for his tribe: "Soon after our return to Fort Wrangell this grand old man was killed in a quarrel in which he had taken no other part than that of peacemaker."⁶⁶ Instead of going to fight, Toyatte carried no weapon at all, but rather went in the battlefield to cheer and rouse his companions. True enough, Chief Toyatte was a former slaveholder, but his final sacrifice more than made up for, in Muir's mind, this deficiency.

In his Journal, edited by Linnie Marsh Wolfe under the title *John of the Mountains*, Muir comments on the altruistic nature of the Pacific Northwest potlatch: "Occasionally a rich Indian holds a grand potlatch, giving away all the hard-earned savings of a lifetime. Then he becomes a chief on Tyee. A good way to get rid of riches in old age when from their kind they are hard to keep. It is the common price of fame and power."⁶⁷ Materialism was hardly a sin for this group of Indians. Alcoholism, introduced by whites as a device to take advantage of Tlingits, was a weakness, but certainly not the materialism so prevalent in Euro-American civilization. They were a spiritual people, as Muir points out: "A spirit was embodied in every mountain, stream and waterfall."⁶⁸

Muir addressed himself to this spirituality, as Young explains in *Alaska Days with John Muir*, by telling "the eager natives wonderful things about what the great one God, whose name is love, was doing for them."⁶⁹ Muir's preaching universal religion to the Indians and his constant search for new glaciers earned him the title of Glate Ankow (Ice Chief) according to Young. They liked to listen to the Ice Chief as much as to the Reverend Samuel Young, and as Linnie Marsh Wolfe explains, Muir gave five sermons of his own (one of these sermons is in the Appendix of this study) at a Chilcat village "in which he told them all men were brothers, regardless of color or race. They were so delighted with the Ice Chief that they begged him to come back and be their teacher. If he did, old and young would go to school. As an inducement they offered him a native wife."⁷⁰ However, Muir refused the offer because he was already engaged to Miss Louie Strentzel, but as he wrote of his Tlingit friends, "I seem to be among old friends with whom I had long been acquainted, though I have never been here before."[71] Such a statement is in marked contrast to his reflection in *My First Summer in the Sierra*, "Perhaps if I knew them better, I should like them better."[72]

I do not mean to imply that Muir found nothing bad in the Tlingits of Alaska. He strongly disapproved of slaveholding, fratricidal battles, and alcoholism. While at a Hootsenoo village, Muir noted that "The whole village was afire with bad whiskey. This was the first time in my life that I learned the meaning of the phrase, 'a howling drunk.' Even our Indians hesitated to venture alone, not withstanding whiskey storms were far from novel to them."[73] On Muir's second trip to Alaska in 1880 he did not fail to give a sharp reprimand to an Indian traveling companion who wantonly killed a seagull: "I asked him why he had killed the bird, and followed the questions by a severe reprimand for his stupid cruelty, to which he could offer no other excuse than that he had learned from the whites to be careless about taking life."[74] Nonetheless, Muir's overall impressions of Tlingit culture were strongly positive, so much so that he became one of them in spirit, and they even grew to understand and appreciate his extreme fascination for the remote and sublime wilderness of glaciers and mountain peaks.

To feel completely at home with a different people is to experience, in part, a oneness with them. Muir was brought back to his boyhood in bonny Scotland by experiencing such simple joys as eating sliced raw turnips with the Indians. And when Muir stayed with an Indian chief on Admiralty Island, he "never felt more at home. The loving kindness bestowed on the little ones made the house glow."[75] On the way to Glacier Bay northwest of present-day Juneau, a bad storm frightened Muir's Indian friends, Kadachan and Toyatte. To illustrate how much Muir had become part of Indian culture, I quote the following passage describing his words of cheer and their effect:

They seemed to be losing heart with every howl of the wind, and, fearing that they might fail me now that I was in the midst of so grand a congregation of glaciers, I made haste to reassure them, telling them that for ten years I had wandered alone among mountains and storms, and good luck always followed me; that with me, therefore, they need fear nothing. The storm would soon cease and the sun would shine to show us the way we should go, for God cares for us and guides us as long as we are trustful and brave, therefore all childish fear must be put away. This little speech did good. Kadachan, with some show of enthusiasm, said he liked to travel with good-luck people; and dignified old Toyatte declared that now his heart was strong again, and he would venture on with me as far as I liked for my "wawa" was "delait" (my talk was very good). The old warrior even became a little sentimental, and said that even if the canoe was broken he would not greatly care, because on the way to the other world he would have good companions.[76]

And it wasn't long until the Indians with Muir began to take delight in things they never before enjoyed like seeing glaciers for the sake of it and hearing the roar of icebergs breaking off into lonely bays. One old chief whom Muir met on his third trip to Alaska (recorded in *Travels in Alaska*) actually stripped off his dry clothes and put on wet ones in sympathy for this white friend who continued on into stormy and drenched glacial fjords.

John Muir had to overcome some few stringent preconceptions of Indian people to love and respect his Tlingit friends. The fact that he did admire his Maidu Indian working companion in 1869, and that he developed a deep respect for the Alaskan natives (including Yup'iks as we shall see), leads me to believe that had he become acquainted with the more "fearful" Plains Indian tribes (who were not as recent immigrants to North America as were the Alaskans as he notes in *Travels in Alaska*), he may very well have grown fond of them too.[77] Through somebody like Black Elk of the Oglala Sioux, Muir would have gained at least an equal admiration for Plains cultures' land wisdom. The fact that Black Elk held Mother Earth to be sacred, as expressed in his visionary autobiography *Black Elk Speaks* (recorded by John G. Neihardt), leads me to assume that Muir and Black Elk would have been spiritual brothers. Their metaphysical views of the universe are strikingly parallel in their recognition of a spiritual harmony to which man must attune himself or fail in this life.

But the Tlingits, and not Black Elk, taught Muir that happiness in one's original environment is a true key to ecological wisdom. To be happy in a place is to be one with it. If a new settler or immigrant to a strange land cannot develop a sense of happiness, he will probably leave for some other place. Tlingits took delight in simplistic wilderness living in their native panhandle Alaska. As he wrote in *Travels in Alaska*, "There can be no happiness in this world or in any other for those who may not be happy here."[78] The Tlingits were basically a merry people; one need only recall Kadachan's laughter over his own bungling attempts to retrieve a shot duck. Laughter and happiness connote inner harmony so essential to outer harmony. But many problems introduced by white men have caused sadness. Muir, like our own contemporary Arctic Scotsman Duncan Pryde, expressed a deep concern for the protection of the rights of these Northern peoples:

Unprincipled whiskey-laden traders are their bane; common-sense Christian teachers their greatest blessing. A few good missionaries, a few good cannon with men behind them, and fair play, protection from whiskey, is all the Alaska Indians require. Uncle Sam has no better subjects, white, black or brown, or any more deserving his considerate care.[79]

Let us turn to the 1881 journey to Arctic Alaska as recorded in *The Cruise of the Corwin*.

## TRAVELS IN ARCTIC ALASKA AND SIBERIA

Herbert F. Smith, in his book *John Muir*, asserts that the visiting Scotsman's observations on Yup'ik and Chukchi cultures are merely superficial:

JOHN MUIR'S SKETCH OF A YUP'IK GIRL
(HITHERTO UNPUBLISHED).

A return to the old situation no longer being possible, Muir urges that the government complete the process of civilization for the Eskimos [Yup'iks], taking them out of the balance of nature in their environment entirely. Nobody who has read any of Muir's other books could possibly believe that this solution seems ideal to him; but, the degradation of the Eskimo having become an accomplished fact, he can see no other course of action possible. [80]

However, because Muir's commentary, like that of Duncan Pryde, suggests that Arctic solutions to Arctic problems can be found, his views cannot be labeled superficial. As Smith points out, Muir fully sympathized with the wilderness way of life which was gravely threatened by forces of civilization. But, rather than completing the process of civilizing Yup'iks and Chuckchis, Muir, I believe, advocates a maintenance of Arctic cultures through northern not southern resources.

John Muir agreed in 1881 to sail aboard the *Corwin*, whose fruitless mission it was to search for the missing whaler *Jeannette*. (It is curious to note that Thoreau, too, had Arctic interests as evidenced by his reading and note-taking from such books as John Richardson's *Arctic Searching Expedition*, 1852; Sherard Osborn's *Stray Leaves from an Arctic Journal*, 1852; and David Crantz's *The History of Greenland*, 1767; but Thoreau never traveled to the Arctic.) Muir's cruise would afford him the opportunity to examine evidence of living glaciation on the Arctic coastlines of Siberia and Alaska. While much attention is paid to such evidence, an important element in the book concerns the living conditions and lifestyle of Alaskan Yup'iks and Siberian Chukchis. On the way north, Muir first encounters the Unanga^x people, who "are far more civilized and Christianized than any other tribe of Alaska Indians."[81] Despite the fact that they are successful hunters and fishers and have the ingenuity of adapting to the modern world by doing such things as making arrowheads out of glass bottle fragments, unfortunately, "They are fading away like other Indians. The deaths exceed the births in nearly every one of their villages, and it is only a question of time when they will vanish from the face of the earth" (P. 14). It must be pointed out that to note Unanga^x are vanishing is not quite the same thing as to *advocate* the process. The main problem with the Unanga^x, despite the strength of their traditional religion and Shamanism, from Muir's point of view, is the white man's introduction of alcohol:

As the Tlingit Indians of the Alexander Archipelago make their own whiskey, so these Aleuts [Unanga^x] make their own beer, an intoxicating drink, which, if possible, is more abominable and destructive than hootchenoo. It is called "Kvass," and was introduced by the Russians, though the Aleutian kvass is only a coarse imitation of the Russian article, as the Indian hootchenoo is of whiskey. (Pp. 15–16)

Muir goes on to say that Unanga^x will spend their hard-earned pay obtained by fishing and hunting on drink, and he mentions one poor chap would have gladly given his $800 bank account for five bottles of whiskey (P. 20).

As the *Corwin* sailed north, Muir met his first Yup'ik at the northwestern end of Saint Lawrence Island in the Bering Sea. One of the most striking characteristics of these people was their happiness despite the dreary environment: "It was blowing and snowing at the same time, and the poor storm-beaten row of huts seemed inexpressedly dreary through the drift. Nevertheless, out of them came a crowd of jolly, well fed people dragging their skin canoes, which they shoved over the rim of stranded ice that extended along the shore . . ." (P. 26).

They wanted to trade for rum, rifles, and cartridges, and, as Muir notes, "There seems to be no good reason why common rifles should be prohibited, inasmuch as they would surely and easily gain a living by their use" (P. 27). By "common rifles" Muir means nonrepeating ones. Certainly he is advocating that Saint Lawrence Yup'iks should continue as hunters and fishermen, only they should use common rifles instead of harpoons and spears. If alcohol interferes with this process, something must be done: "As to alcohol, no restriction can possibly be too stringent. To the Yup'ik it is misery and oftentimes quick death. Two years ago the inhabitants of several villages on this island died of starvation caused by abundance of rum, which rendered them careless about the laying up of ordinary supplies of food for the winter" (P. 21). For Muir, forces inherent in civilization disrupt existing natural harmonies. Far from implying that Saint Lawrence Yup'iks should be absorbed by the civilization, as Smith contends, Muir is advocating stringent embargoes on the cheap commercialization of Arctic cultures. There is something, however, within the Yup'ik's being that counteracts civilization's bad influences and that is his merry, happy-go-lucky nature: "Always searching for something to laugh at, the (Yup'iks) are ready to stop short in the middle of the most important bargainings to get hold of some bit of fun" (P. 29). Without their inherent happiness and good humor, Yup'iks might have been completely annihilated by the white man of Muir's day.

Shortly after the *Corwin* docked on the Siberian peninsula in search of the lost *Jeannette*, Muir met his first Chukchi natives. They had few material possessions, "Yet they seemed more confident of their ability to earn a living than most whites on their farms" (P. 32). This is a rather telling statement. In fact, of all the Yup'ik people, the Chukchis seemed, to Muir, the most self-sufficient. The captain of the *Corwin* employed Chukchi Joe as a guide to help search for the crew of the *Jeannette*, and it was through this man that Muir became more intimately acquainted with Chukchi living. Upon seeing the guide's little hut, Muir remarked, "After being out all day hunting in the stormy weather, or on icepacks or frozen tundras, the Chukchi withdraws into his furry sanctum, takes off all his clothing and spreads his wearied limbs in luxurious ease, sleeping perfectly nude in the severest weather" (P. 35). His home is made all the more comfortable by a unique moss and oil lamp giving his hut a soft, warm glow. Muir constantly marveled at these natives' ability to make do with little in the severest climate of our planet. Native contented adaptiveness is the key to his environmental harmony.

In addition to admiring their simplicity of living, Muir grew to understand and appreciate inner qualities of the Chukchi people. When their guide parted from his wife to participate in the search, Muir comments: "One touch of nature makes all the world kin, and there were many touches among the wild Chukchis" (P. 36). And it was among the "wild Chukchis" that Muir grew to appreciate the powers of expression and mannerly reserve not readily discernible in white civilization. Traveling on to Saint Lawrence Bay, Siberia, Muir and company met the old orator Jaroochah, whom he described as a "remarkable" man with a voice more powerful than a gale or volcano. Muir had the unique opportunity to watch Jaroochah in action:

The old orator poured fourth his noisy eloquence late and early, like a perennial mountain spring, some of his deep chest tones sounding in a storm like the roar of the lion. He rolled his wolfish

eyes and tossed his brown skinny limbs in a frantic storm of gestures, now suddenly foreshortening himself to less than half his
height, then shooting aloft with Jack-in-the-box rapidity, while
his people looked on and listened, apparently half in fear, half in
admiration. (P. 61)

One can sense that Jaroochah gained Muir's respect as well.

The visiting Scotsman could not help but notice the "unhastening
dignity" of these people when food was set before them. He observed that
even the children restrained themselves from grabbing food like the hungry poor among the whites. Muir comments:

Even when a year of famine occurs from any cause, they endure it
with fortitude such as would be sought for in vain among the civilized, and after braving the most intense of these dreary icebound
coasts in search of food, if unsuccessful, they wrap themselves in
their furs and die quietly as if only going to sleep. (Pp. 37–38)

Here *The Cruise of the Corwin* interestingly foreshadows Jack London's fascinating story "The Law of Life," which focuses upon Arctic stoicism and
self-sacrifice.

While searching for the crew of the *Jeanette* aboard a dogsled, Muir
marveled at the Chukchis' mastery of travel over the roughest terrain
imaginable with plunges and pitches like a roller coaster: "It was a rare,
strange ride for us, yet accomplished with such everyday commonplace
confidence, that it seemed at the time as if this might be the only mode of
travel in the world" (P. 43). Here was a clear example of Chukchi adaptivity
to the land. They did not fight against the land but seemed to join with it.

One of the most important aspects of Chukchis' self-sufficiency was
reindeer herding. Muir observes:

The reindeer is found throughout the Arctic and subarctic regions
of both Asia and America, and, in either the wild or domestic state

supplies to the natives an abundance of food and warm clothing, thus rendering these bleak and intensely cold regions inhabitable. I believe it is only in Lapland and Siberia that the reindeer is domesticated. (P. 140)

Muir is quite surprised that the Yup'iks of North America do not follow the example of the Chukchis; "no domesticated herds are found on the American continent, though the natives have illustration enough of their value on the opposite shores of the Bering Sea" (P. 139). Is not John Muir here implying much the same solution as Duncan Pryde advocates in his book *Nunaga*? Pryde believes that Arctic resources must be widely used by Arctic people, including the herding of such animals as caribou and musk oxen. *The Cruise of the Corwin* illustrates that while natives wantonly slaughtered reindeer with the excuse that the deer spirit would be offended if he was not killed when in abundance (probably an excuse made since the coming of white men with the inducement of alcohol and quick dollars), the Chukchis thought more of the future by herding. Muir remarks that "they are not savage by any means, however, but steady, industrious workers, looking well ahead, providing for the future, and consequently seldom in want, save when at long intervals disease or other calamities overtake their herds" (P. 228). By innuendo Muir is suggesting the viable solution to Arctic survival of herding which was, during the late 1880s, actually adopted by native Alaskans.[82]

At the Diomede Island, Muir was flabbergasted by the villages of the dead where hundreds perished from famine shortly before the searching expedition of the *Corwin*. As he looked around at scores of dead bodies strewn here and there, the islanders told Muir that all were "dead," "all mucky," "all gone." It is at this point where Muir reacts forcefully:

Unless some aid be extended by our government which claims these people, in a few years at most every soul of them will have vanished from the face of the earth; for, even where alcohol is left out of the count, the few articles of food, clothing, guns,

etc., furnished by the traders, exert a degrading influence, making them less self-reliant, and less skillful as hunters. They seem
susceptible of civilization, and well deserve the attention of our
government. (P. 122)

Muir would be in agreement with Francis Jennings's thesis that Indians of
the Americas have been culturally raped by Europeans. As Jennings writes
in his 1976 book, *The Invasion of America*:

No slaughter was impermissible, no lie dishonorable, no breach
of trust shameful, if it advantaged the champions of true religion.
In the gradual transition from religious conceptions to racial
conceptions, the gulf between persons calling themselves Christian and the other persons, whom they called heathen, translated
smoothly into a chasm between whites and coloreds. The law of
moral obligation sanctioned behavior on only one side of that
chasm.[83]

However, Muir himself subscribed to no such bigotry and had some faith
that the US government of the 1880s could be persuaded to act on the principles of Christ and *not* of people claiming to be Christians. Herbert F.
Smith, I believe, misreads this important passage by assuming Muir wants
the government to continue the process of degradation and dependency
rather than the reverse. *Because* these natives are susceptible to the forces
of civilization and because they are being rendered less self-reliant, our
government must act. It was not only in Alaska that Muir saw the degrading effects of civilization. In his essay "Hunting Big Redwoods" published
in 1901 in *Atlantic Monthly* (and later in *Our National Parks*), he describes
his encounter with an Indian shepherd who wondered if he was searching for gold. Muir asked him questions about the wilderness "but unfortunately he proved to be a tame Indian from the Tule Reservation, had
been to school, claimed to be civilized, and spoke contemptuously of 'wild
Indians,' and so of course his inherited instincts were blurred or lost."[84]

Making the Indian feel ashamed of his own people is the lowest form of degradation. But in Alaska our government can and should act, demands Muir. One specific action concerns rifles: "Common rifles would be better for them, partly on account of the difficulty of obtaining supplies of cartridges, and partly because repeating rifles tempt them to destroy large amounts of game which they do not need. The reindeer have in this manner been well-nigh exterminated within the last few years" (Pp. 133–34). Herding and not overkilling seems to be the most sensible Arctic policy. White man's alcoholic crippling of the native's natural penchant for surviving well for countless generations was one of the worst crimes ever committed.

In addition to potential self-sufficiency (an admired Emersonian tenet) and a merry nature, dwellers of the Arctic were a very loving and caring people: "No happier baby could be found in warm parlors, where loving attendants anticipate every want and the looms of the world afford their best in the way of soft fabrics" (P. 75). Muir watched a peaceful Yup'ik baby go to sleep with snowflakes falling gently in its face, and he reflected:

These people interest me greatly, and it is worth coming far to know them, however slightly. The smile, or rather, broad grin of the Eskimo [Yup'ik] baby went directly to my heart, and I shall remember it as long as I live. When its features had subsided into perfect repose, the laugh gone from its dark eyes, and the lips closed over its two teeth, I could make its sweet smile bloom out again as often as I nodded and chirruped to it. Heaven bless it! Some of the boys, too, lads from eight to twelve years of age, were well-behaved, bashful, and usually laughed and turned away their faces when looked at. But there was a response in their eyes which made you feel that they are your brothers. (Pp. 76–77)

Like Willa Cather in *Death Comes for the Archbishop*, Muir strongly admired native architectural accommodation to local environments. Cather admired Navajo hogans being made of sand and willows and Muir marveled at Yup'ik huts which were "picturesque and daring beyond conception" (P. 111). In fact, the huts he observed at Diomede Island seemed:

> the queerest human nests conceivable. They are simply light, square frames made of drift poles gathered on the beach, and covered with walrus hide that has been carefully dressed and stretched tightly on the frame like the head of a drum. The skin is of a yellow color, and white translucent, so that when in one feels as if one were inside a huge blown bladder, the light sifting in through the skin at the top and all around, yellow as sunset. The entire establishment is window, one pane for the roof, which is also the ceiling, and for each of the four sides, without cross sash-bars to mar the brave simplicity of it all. (P. 237)

Muir took particular delight in Arctic people's novel use of nature for their homes, something he himself did when he built his cabin in Yosemite in which frogs creeped through the slats of the floor to serenade him each evening as he wrote at his desk.

Muir noticed with fascination that Chukchis killed their reindeer reverently and ceremoniously. He describes such a ceremony reminiscent of Pueblo deer-killing rituals depicted by Frank Waters in the novel *The Man Who Killed the Deer*:

> After it [the reindeer] was slain they laid it on its side. One of the women brought forward a branch of willow about a foot long, with the green leaves on it, and put it under the animal's head. Then she threw four or five handfuls of the blood, from the knife-wound back of the shoulder, making me get out of the way, as if this direction were the only proper one. Next she took a cupful of water and poured a little on its mouth and tail and on the wound. While this ceremony was being performed all the family looked serious, but as soon as it was over they began to laugh and chat as before. (P. 234).

True reverence for all life strongly appealed to John Muir. For both the Indians and Muir there exists a spiritual bond between humans and animals. He was delighted to discover that Indians believed that animals and humans share the next world as well as this one; as he notes in *John of the Mountains*, "Indian dogs go to the Happy Hunting Grounds with their masters."[85] Muir, himself, had similar sympathies as early as his boyhood days in Wisconsin.

Despite the fact that Arctic natives had some rather severe problems to overcome, including alcoholism, a ready susceptibility to the forces of civilization, and a lack of understanding of the environmental consequences of using repeating rifles to overkill, they were for John Muir a people worthy of deep respect and concern. Unlike some of the lying, cheating, and stealing intruders into the Arctic, they were joyous and simple in the Thoreauvian sense. Muir's final estimate of native peoples comes near the close of *The Cruise of the Corwin*:

The extent of the dealings of these people, usually regarded as savages, is truly surprising. And that they can keep warm and make a living on this bleak, fog-smothered, storm-beaten [land], and have time to beget, feed and train children, and give them a good Yup'ik education; that they teach them to shoot the bow, to make and throw the bird spears, to make and use those marvelous kayaks to kill seals, bears, and wolves, to hunt and whale, capture the different kinds of fishes, manufacture different sorts of leather, dress skins and make them into clothing, besides teaching them to carry on trade, to make fire by rubbing two pieces of wood together, and to build the strange house—that they can do all this, and still have time to be sociable, to dance, sing, gossip, and discuss ghosts, spirits, and all the nerve-racking marvels of the shaman world, shows how truly wild, and brave, and capable a people these . . . Eskimos [Yup'iks] are. (Pp. 238–39)

It is clearly evident that John Muir believed native people lived harmoniously on the land before the coming of the white man and that he was highly critical of white intrusion into the Arctic which brought alcohol, repeating rifles, and other items which disrupted previously sound ecological relationships.

Muir's Alaskan experience did have a profound impact on his environmental philosophy developed in *The Mountains of California*, which was written after his contact with Tlingit and Yup'ik cultures. In the second edition of *The Mountains of California*, Muir lashes out at those forces in "civilization" which tend to disrupt natural harmonies. What he had seen happening in the Arctic he saw happening in his own beloved California at the turn of the century. Of the Hetch Hetchy dam proposal, Muir sounds like an early day Edward Abbey in *The Monkey Wrench Gang* or *Desert Solitaire*: "These temple destroyers, devotees of ravaging commercialism, seem to have a perfect contempt for Nature, and, instead of lifting their eyes to the God of the mountains, lift them to the Almighty Dollar."[86] Native Alaskan cultures were, for him, a marked contrast, and they confirmed his belief that a viable alternative lifestyle was possible. They had much to teach to a man who was willing to learn. Muir was surely among those conservationists who, as Stephen Fox in *John Muir and His Legacy* puts it, "found their own people deficient—stupid at best, perhaps willfully selfish and shortsighted, in any case less wise than the native populations they displaced."[87]

# A Postscript on Thoreau and and Muir

Nature was *the way* for Thoreau and Muir; it led them to spiritual truths found along the shores of Walden Pond, the heights of Mount Katahdin, the depths of the Sierra Redwoods, and the glacial summits of Alaskan peaks. Thoreau's and Muir's vital contact with American Indians of Maine and Alaska greatly enriched their understanding of the spirituality of nature, making it an even more significant way through this side of life. While they did not have Zen masters to guide them in some Oriental temple, they did have wilderness "masters" adept in the rich art of deciphering nature's code for purposes of living a viable alternative lifestyle close to the American land. As Kiowa author N. Scott Momaday admonishes in *The Way to Rainy Mountain*, a man ought to familiarize himself with a particular landscape of his choosing, to get to know it in all its moods, "to be taken up" by it until it intermingles with his very being.

.

Henry David Thoreau and John Muir's
Unpublished Manuscripts on Primal Cultures
of the American Wilderness

I.

As stated earlier in this study, Thoreau began taking notes on Indian cultures in 1847 and continued to do so through his trip to Minnesota during the spring of 1861. The fragmentary unpublished essay which here follows was probably written in late 1852 or early 1853.[1] He had not yet met Joe Aitteon or Joe Polis, who aided Thoreau immeasurably in his Indian education deep in the Maine Woods. Therefore this essay is at best ambivalent in its appraisal of primal cultures. Thoreau, for instance, fully appreciates civilization's link (the drum, place-names like Chicago) with a primal past, yet he seems to disdain earth-mound cultures which have no military roads or monuments like those of the Aztecs or Incas. The notes which follow are reproduced with permission from the Pierpont Morgan Library and are in chronological order.

## THOREAU'S FRAGMENTARY ESSAY ON PRIMAL CULTURE

The Medicine man is indispensable to work upon the imagination of the Indian by his jugglery—and of like value for the most part as the physician to the civilized man.

Men lived and died in America, though they were copper colored, before the white man came. Charlevoix states that the Olchagnas, commonly called Puana—who gave their name to the Baye de Puans (Green Bay) already much reduced lost 600 of their best men in a single squawl.

Whence, it is that all nations have something like a drum. Charlevoix speaks of the *tambour* of the Indians. There would appear to be a kind of necessity in human nature to produce this instrument. In London & Paris you hear the sound of the unmusical drum which has come down from antiquity.

The trader's price for a handkerchief or string of beads in California is all the gold the Indian has got be it more or less—a thousand dollars is not too much *nor* one dollar too little. Accordingly the Indian learns to put his gold into separate little sacks, and say that one contains his all.—So was it with the fur traders. [111]

How tan [a French explorer] returning from his somewhat fabulous expedition up the River *Longue* in 1688 says "We arrived there for the 24th at *Chekakou* (Chicago), the place where the reembarkment was to be made." Thus the white man has but followed in the steps of the Indian. Where the Ind. made his portages the white man makes his—or makes the stream more navigable. The New Englander goes to Wisconsin & Iowa by routes which the Indians discovered & used ages ago—and partly perchance the buffaloes used before the Indians. At the points of embarkation or debarkation in the route where was once an Indian is now in many instances no doubt a white man's city—with its wharves. [Interestingly enough, this is a major point made by the modern historian Francis Jennings in his book *The Invasion of America.*]

Labor among the Indians was to a certain extent merely mechanically divided between men & women. The former making their canoes and nets [,] traps &c—whatever [their?] hunting & fishing required—The women—made the utensils of the house &c.

Each savage feels the necessity of being governed by reason in the absence of law—Hence gives of his game to his 'old relations' &c.

The Indian like the muskrat fee(d) on fresh water clams apparently—Both had a strong hold on life naturally—but are alike exterminated at last by the white man's improvements. He was hardy & supple & of a cold temperament like the muskrat whose feast he shared and whose skins he often used. [112]

What a vast difference between a savage & a civilized people. At first it appears but a slight difference in degree—and the savage excelling in many physical qualities—we underrate the comparative general superiority of the civilized man. Compare the American family (so called by Morton), with (his) Toltecan—Consider what kind of relics the former have left—at most rude earthen mounds—pottery, & stone implements; but of the latter Morton says, "From the Rio Gila in California, to the southern extremity of Peru, their architectural remains are every where encountered to surprise the traveller and confound the antiquary: among these are pyramids, temples, grotoes, bas-relifs, and arabesques; while their roads, aquaducts and fortifications, and the sites of their mining operations, sufficiently attest their attainments in the practical arts of life."

How different the evidence afforded by an earthen mound containing rude fragments of pottery & stone spearheads—and that afforded the remains of a public or military road.

Morton (in his *Crania*) quotes Sir Wm Jones [indirectly] as saying "The Greeks called all the southern nations of the world by the common appellation of Ethiopians. Thus using Ethiop and Indian as convertable terms." Being the origin of the word "Indian"? [113]

Perhaps what the Orientals were to the Greeks—barbarians—the Indians are to some extent to us.

We have a voluminous history of Europe for the last 10,000

years—Suppose we had as complete a history of Mexico & Peru
for the same period—a history of the American Continent,—the
reverse of the medal. It is hard to believe they, a civilised people,
inhabited these countries unknown to the old world! What kind
of facts—what kind of events are those which transpired in America before it was known to the inhabitants of the old world?

"The archaeological antiquaries, without reference to any
theory derived from mythology or from languages, have found
that their subjects of study, the relics of antiquity, naturally fall
into three divisions:—that of an age prior to the use of metals in
arms or utensils, when bone & stone were the materials used; and
in that age burning appears to have been the way of disposing of
the dead, less perhaps from any observance connected with religion, than from the want of metal tools to dig the soil with so as
to inter the dead;—that is a mixture of metals to give hardness
to copper or other soft metals; and in which age the use of stone
for hammers, arrow-points, or spearheads, [114] was still mixed
with the use of metals; and lastly an age when iron was applied
to these purposes, although bronze, and even stone & bone, were
still in use, from the want no doubt, of a sufficient supply of iron,
and from the great consumpt of it in missile weapons. Although
dates cannot be assigned to these three ages, and they run into
each other, yet the mass of relics of ancient times so clearly fall
into these three divisions, that the Museum of Northern Antiq-
uities at Copenhagen is divided & arranged upon this principle,
and with the fullest approbation of the learned antiquaries of the
North. The division coincides with & confirms the results of the
mythological and philological researches. These epochs, however,
are beyond the pale of chronology." Laing's Appendix to Jnorrs?
*[Journal of Residence in Norway]*

In Kin Hakon, the Broad-shouldered's fleet in the 12th century—"All the small ships lay farther off, and they were all nearly
loaded with weapons & stones." Jnorrs.

King Sigfried the Crusader of Norway earlier the same century "imposed a duty on all the districts in the neighborhood of
the town [of Konghelle], as well as on the town's people,—that
every person of nine years of age and upwards should bring to
the castle five missile stones for weapons, or as many large stakes,
sharp at one end and 5 ells long." Ibid [115]

The Indians having no Sunday-feasts, games dance &c, are
the more important to them!

The recent '52 persecution in Persia of the Sect of the Babis
equals in the atrocity of the tortures employed—the lingering
deaths at which all people assist—the practices of our Indians. [116]

*Indian Notebooks* VI, MA 601, Pp. 111–16

Thoreau's notes from Henry Roe Schoolcraft's *History of the Indian Tribes of
the United States* (1851–1857) in six volumes are characterized by whimsical
tales, the importance of the seasons to Indians, and the importance of friendship and unity as evidenced by Chief Hiawatha. Notes from Schoolcraft here
follow. It is important to observe that *Indian Notebooks* volumes V and VI
were written by Thoreau in the early 1850s. Volumes VII and VIII were written in the mid-1850s and IX, X, and XI in the late 1850s and early 1860s.

From The Magic Circle in the Prairie: "A young hunter found
a circular path one day in a prairie without any trail leading to
or from it." He hid himself in the grass & found that 12 beautiful girls came down from heaven (in) an osier cart with music, &
leaping out began to dance. He tried in many occasions to seize
the youngest & finally by changing himself into a mouse succeeded. He took her home to his lodge & she bore him a beautiful boy. But she was the daughter of a star "and the scenes of
earth began to fall upon her sight, wished to visit her father." "She
remembered the dream that would carry her up" so one day when
Algon was hunting she constructed a wicker basket—took her
son to the charmed ring—commenced her song & rose into the

skies—The sound of her singing was wafted to her husband's ear, but he arrived too late to detain them.

She finally returned for her husband—but they all at length returned to earth in the form of white hawks which they still retain.

*Indian Notebooks* V, MA 600, Pp. 104, 105

"The genii and spirits who inhabit the solid ground are covered, during the winter season, by beds of snow, and the lakes and rivers with ice, which make them insensible to hearing. The fanciful & grotesque tales that are told in the winter lodge, where the old and young are crowded together, often produce jeers and remarks from the listeners, and create merriment which would be offensive to the genii if they were overheard."

"As soon as the spring opens . . . these tales cease. The earth is now seminated. The snows disappear, the lakes & rivers open, the birds return to their deserted forests or streams, the leaves put forth, it is now that the spirit world in which the Indians live, assumes its most intense state of activity, and the red hunter who believes himself dependent on the spirits and genii for success in every path of life, is regardful of the least word which might give offense to these newly awakened powers." [Here again we see Thoreau's interest in the rich linkage between the Indian's language and nature.]

*Indian Notebooks* VII, MA 602, Pp. 204–5

"Hiawatha, or the Origin of the Onandaga Council Fire" (Derived from the verbal narrations of the late Abraham Le Fort, an Onandaga Chief, who was a graduate, it is believed, of Geneva College.) "Tarenyawago taught the Six Nations arts & knowledge. He had a canoe which could move without paddles. It was only necessary to wish it, to compel it to go. With this he ascended the streams & lakes. He taught the people to raise corn & beans, removed obstructions from their water courses and made their fishing-grounds clear. He helped to get the mastery over the great monsters which over ran the country, and thus prepared the forests for their hunters. His wisdom was as great as his power. The people listened to him with admiration and followed his advice gladly. There was nothing in which he did not excel good hunters, brave warriors, and eloquent orators."

"He gave them wise instructions for observing the laws and maxims of the Great Spirit. Having done these things, he laid aside the high powers of his public missions, and resolved to set them an example of how they should live. For this purpose, he selected a beautiful spot (on the shores of a lake) erected his lodge—planted his field of corn, kept by him his magic canoe, and selected a wife & dropt his old name & took that of Hiawatha, meaning a person of very great wisdom," was very much respected & consulted— became a member of the Onandaga tribe & only used his 'magic canoe' when he went to attend councils. At length there arose suddenly great alarm at the invasion of a fierce band of warriors from the north of the Great Lakes. The council was assembled, Hiawatha was sent. He arrived. (Then a story of the fall of something like a meteor one would say . . .—but it was called a great white bird[.]) He advised the tribes to unite into band—"Listen to me by tribes.

"You (the Mohawks), who are sitting under the shadow of the Great Tree, whose roots sink deep in the earth . . . and whose branches spread wide around, shall be the first nation, because you are war-like & mighty."

[Thoreau's notes on the Oneydoes (second nation) are illegible.]

"You (the Onandagas), who have your habitation at the foot of the Great Hills, and are overshadowed by their crags, shall be the third nation, because you are all greatly gifted in speech.

"You (the Senecas), whose dwelling is in the Dark Forest, and whose home is everywhere, shall be the fourth nation, because of your superior aiming in hunting."

"And you (the Cayugas), the people who live in the Open Country, and possess much wisdom, shall be the fifth nation, because you understand better the art of raising corn and beans, and making house."

"Unite, you 5 nations, and have one common interest, and no foe shall disturb & subdue you. You, the people who are as the public wishes, and you, who are a fishing people may place yourselves under our protection, and we will defend you. And you of the south & of the west may do the same, and we will protect you. We earnestly desire the attention & friendship of you all."

"Brothers, if we unite in this great band, the Great Spirit will smile upon us, and we shall be free, prosperous, & happy. But if we remain as we are, we shall be subject to his frown. We shall be enslaved, ruined, perhaps, annihilated. We may perish under the war-storm, and our names be no longer remembered by good men, not be repeated in the dance & song."

"Brothers, these are the words of Hiawatha, I have said it. I am done." He took his scat [he took his leave] in his canoe—music was heard in the air—& he disappeared in the heavens. [Thoreau, perhaps, saw natural harmony in Hiawatha's words which was in marked contrast to the state of his own nation at the time.]

*Indian Notebooks* VII, MA 602, Pp. 185–88.

As one would expect, Thoreau's notes from the multivolumed seventeenth-century *Jesuit Relations* (1632–1673) concern richly poetic mythic origins and, more importantly, religious beliefs of Algonquin Indians about the afterlife.

*[Jesuit Relations of 1635]*
"They [Hurons] say that a certain woman named Eataentsic, is that one who has made the earth & men. They give her for associate a certain one called Iouskeha, who they say is her grandson, with whom she governs the world; this Iouskeha has care of the living & things which concern life, and consequently they say that

he is good. Eataentsic has care of souls, and because they think that she makes men die, they say she is bad. And there are among their mysteries so concealed that is only the old men who can speak for them with credit & authority to be believed."

"Eataentsic fell from heaven—and when she fell she was enceinte [pregnant]."

*Indian Notebooks* VI, MA 601, Pp. 77–78

*[Jesuit Relations of 1636]*

A certain woman Ataentsic working in her field in heaven saw a bear—her dog persued[,] she after & all fell through a hole to earth (or rather water) which afterward became dry—she being pregnant[.]

*Indian Notebooks* VI, MA 601, P. 96

*[Jesuit Relations of 1636]*

Others say that her husband was sick & thinking it would heal him to cut the tree on which they all lived in heaven, she struck it for him, it tumbled down here, she jumped after, the tortoise saw her coming, advised the animals to dive & bring up earth & pile it on his back in which she was received. She soon brought forth 2 boys Taoiscanon & Toskeha, who quarrelled—for arms[.] The last had a deer's horn; the other son fruits of the wild rose— Iousekaha wounded the other & from his blood were produced stones such as they strike the steel with in France—he finally killed him—This is the origin of the nation.

Others say that in the beginning a man dwelt on an island with a fox & a little animal like a polecat which they call Tsohendaia. The man not liking his confinement asked the fox to dive but he only wetting his paws he threw him in & drowned him—but the other dived so smartly that he hit his nose against the bottom and came up with it covered with mud and thereafter he was so industrious that he increased the isle with all these fields.

Ioskeha is the sun[,] Aetaentsic the moon and their cabin is at
the end of the earth. Tells of young man who went to find the former
who concealed them from the latter who would have injured them.

Others say that first the world was dry & all the water was
under the armpit of a great hog here above[.] Ioskeha got what he
used—at length the latter resolved to make an incision—let out the
water & made all the rivers—lakes—& seas.

Without Ioskeha their kettle would not boil. Who he learned to
make fire from [was] the tortoise. At first he kept the animals shut
up in a great cavern at last concluded to let them out that they might
multiply, but so that he could recover them again. "As they went out
of this cave he wounded all of them in the foot with an arrow, nevertheless the wolf avoided his shot, whence it comes, say they, that
they have the trouble to catch it à la course." He gave them corn &
makes it grow.

"At the feast of the Dead which is made about every 12 years,
souls quit the cemeteries, and as some say are changed into turtle-
doves—but the most common belief is that they go off in company
after this ceremony "covered as they are with robes & collars" to a
great village towards the setting sun—but the old men and children
who can't travel so well remain here in their private villages.—"They
hear sometimes they say the noise of the doors of their cabins, and
the voices of the children who chase the birds from their fields, they
saw corn in its season, and make use of the fields which the living
have abandoned; if some village is burned which often happens
in this country, they are careful to collect from the middle of the
burning the roasted corn and make of it part of their provision."

Of those who go west—each nation has a separate village. "The
souls of those who have died in war make a band apart, the others fear them, and do not permit them to enter their village any-
more than they do the souls of those who have made way with
themselves."

*Indian Notebooks* V, MA 600, Pp. 96–98

*[Jesuit Relations of 1636]*

"Another told me that on the same route [to village of the dead] before arriving at the village, one comes to a cabin, where dwells a certain one named Oseotarach; or Pierce-head (Percé-Teste), who draws the brain from the heads of the dead, & keeps it; it is necessary to pass a river & for all bridge you have only the trunk of a tree fallen across, & supported very slightly. The passage is guarded by a dog who donne le sault to many souls & makes them all off; they are at the same time carried off by the violence of the torrent & drowned."

Some who had been resuscitated told these things to them.

*Indian Notebooks* V, MA 600, P. 98

Notes from David Cusick's *Sketches of Ancient History of the Six Nations* (Lockport, N.Y., 1848) concern the human race's mythic origins:

"Among the ancients there were 2 worlds in existence." The lower world was in a great darkness;—the possession of the great monster; but the upper world was inhabited by mankind; and there was a woman conceived & would have twins born. When her travail drew near, "she lay down on a mattrass & the place sank down with her toward the dark world. The monsters assembled in great alarm—one is appointed to obtain some earth—another to support her. She was received on a great turtle with a little earth on his back[.] While holding here, the turtle increased every moment & became a considerable island of earth, and apparently covered with small bushes." Soon the twins were born & the mother died at once. The turtle became a great island & the children grew up—"one of them possessed with a gentle disposition, and named *Eniogorio*, i.e., the good mind. The other possessed an insolence of character, and was named *Enigonha-hetgea*, i.e., the bad mind." The good mind "was anxious to create a great light in the dark world; but the bad mind was desirous that the world should remain in a natural state." The former out of his parent's head & body created sun, moon & stars. He formed also rivers, plants & animals—especially man, a male & female & "named them *Ea give howe* i.e., a real people." In the meanwhile the bad mind made high *mts*, falls of water, reptiles &c—which the good mind removed again. The bad mind trying to make people succeeded only in making 2 apes—but the good mind afterwards gave them living souls—A note says "It appears by fictitious accounts, that the said beings became civilized people & made their residence in the southern parts of the Island; but afterwards they were destroyed by the barbarous nations, & their fortifications were ruined unto this day." Finally the 2 brothers fight & good mind conquers & destroys the bad mind "and the last words uttered from the bad mind were that he would have equal power over the souls of mankind after death; and he sinks down to eternal doom, and became the Evil Spirit."

The good mind then retired from the earth.

Indian Notebooks IX, MA 604, Pp. 110–11

Thoreau also made notes from the Quaker Indian historian John Heckewelder's *An Account of the History, Manners and Customs of the Indian Nations* (Philadelphia, 1819). In what follows we see notes on mythic origins, the sacredness of animal-human relations, and a prophecy.

"The Indians [Delaware] considered the earth as their universal mother. They believed that they were created within its bosom, where for a long time they had their abode, before they came to live on its surface—as the infant is formed & takes its first growth in the womb of its natural mother."

"Some assert that they lived there in the human shape, while others, with greater consistency, contend that their existence was in the form of certain terrestrial animals, such as the groundhog, the rabbit, & the tortoise. This was their state of preparation, until they were permitted to come out & take their station on this island (a note says, 'The Indians call the Am. cont. an island' &c.) as the Lords of the rest of the creation."

*Indian Notebooks* VII, MA 602, P. 261

"An old Indian told me about 50 years ago, that when he was young, he still followed the custom of his father & ancestors in climbing upon a high mountain or pinnacle, to thank the Great Spirit for all the benefits before bestowed, and to pray for a continuance of his favor."

*Indian Notebooks* VIII, MA 603, Pp. 166–67

"Tradition—That they [Iroquois] had dwelt in the earth where it was dark and where no sun did shine. That though they followed hunting, they ate mice, which they caught with their hands. That *Ganawagahha* (one of them) having accidentally found a hole to get out of the earth at, he went out, and that in walking about on the earth he found a deer, which he took back with him; and that both on account of the meat tasting so very good, and the favorable description he had given them of the country above and on the earth, their mother concluded it best for them all to come out; that accordingly they did so, and immediately set about planting corn, &c. That, however, the *Nocharauorsul*; that is, the groundhog, would not come out but had remained in the ground as before."

*Indian Notebooks* VIII, MA 603, P. 263

". . . in the year 1762 when I resided at Tuscorawas on the Muskingum, I was told by some of them, that there were some animals which Indians did not eat, and among them were the *rabbit* and the *ground-hog*; for, they said, they did not know but that they might be *related* to them! I found also that the Indians, for a similar reason, paid great respect to the rattle snake, whom they called their *grand father*, and would on no account destroy him."

"That the Indians from the earliest times, considered themselves in a manner connected with certain animals, is evident
from various customs still preserved among them, and from the
names of those animals which they have collectively, as well as
individually, assumed. It might, indeed, be supposed that those
animals' names which they have given to their several tribes were
mere badges of distinction, or 'coats of arms' . . . but if we pay
attention to the reasons which they give for those denominations,
the idea of a supposed family connexion is easily discernible.
The tortoise, or as it is commonly called, the *Turtle* tribe, among
the Lenape, claims a superiority & ascendency over the others,
because their relations, the great tortoise, a fabled monster, the
Atlas of their mythology, bears according to their traditions this
great *island* on his back, and also because he is amphibious, and
can live both on land & in the water, which neither of the heads
of the other tribes can do. The merits of the *Turkey*, which gives
its name to the 2d tribe, are that he is stationary, and always
remains with or about them. As to the *Wolf*, after whom the 3d
tribe is named, he is a rambler by nature, running from one place
to another in quest of his prey; yet they consider him as their
benefactor, as it was by his means that the Indians got out of the
interior of the earth. It was he, they believe, who by the appoint-
ment of the Great Spirit, killed the deer whom the Mouse found
who first discovered the way to the surface of the earth, and which
allured them to come out of their damp & dark residence. For that
reason, the wolf is to be honored, and his name preserved forever
among them. Such are their traditions as they were related to me
by an old man of this tribe, more than 50 yrs. ago."

These animals' names are also national badges—coats of
arms—

"The Turtle warrior draws either with a coal or paint here &
there on the trees along the war path, the whole animal carrying

a gun with the muzzle projecting forward, and if he leaves a mark at the place where he has made a stroke on his enemy, it will be the picture of a tortoise. Those of the Turkey tribe paint only one foot of a turkey, and the Wolf tribe, sometimes a wolf at large with one leg & foot raised up to serve as a hand, in which the animal also carries a gun with the muzzle forward. They, however, do not generally use the word 'wolf,' when speaking of their tribe, but call themselves *P'duk-sit*, which means *round*-foot that animal having a round foot like a dog.

*Indian Notebooks* VIII, MA 603, Pp. 263–266

"They are as proud of their origin from the tortoise, the turkey, & the wolf, as the nobles of Europe are of their descent from the feudal barons of ancient times, & when children spring from intermarriages between different tribes, their genealogy is carefully preserved by tradition in the family, that they may know to which tribe they belong."

As for their relations to the animals[,] "They are, in fact, according to their opinions, only the first among equals, the legitimate hereditary sovereigns of the whole animated race, of which they are themselves a constituent part."—Hence distinguish animate & inanimate instead of masculine & feminine. "All animated nature, in whatever degree, is in their eyes a great whole from which they have not yet ventured to separate themselves. They do not exclude other animals from their world of spirits, the place to which they expect to go after death."

"A Delaware hunter once shot a huge bear and broke its backbone. The animal fell and sent up a most plaintive cry, something like that of the panther when he is hungry. The hunter, instead of giving him another shot, stood up close to him, and addressed him in these words: 'Hark ye! bear, you are a coward, and no warrior as you pretend to be. Were you a warrior you would shew it by your firmness and not cry & whimper like an old woman. You

know, bear, that our tribes are at war with each other, and that
yours are the aggressor. [a note says 'probably attending to a tradition which the Indians have of a very ferocious kind of bear, called
the *naked bear*, which &c']—You have found the Indians too powerful for you, and you have gone sneaking about in the woods,
stealing their hogs; perhaps at this time you have hog's flesh in
your belly. Had you conquered me I would have borne it with
courage and died like a brave warrior; but you, bear, sit here & cry,
and disgrace your tribe by your cowardly conduct.' I was present
at the delivery of this curious invective; when the hunter had dis-
patched the bear, I asked him, how he thought that poor animal
could understand what he said to it? 'Oh!' said he in answer, 'the
bear understood me very well; did you not observe how *ashamed*
he looked while I was upbraiding him?' "

He also described another similar scene which he witnessed
among the Wabash.

*Indian Notebooks* VIII, MA 603, Pp. 267–69

"They ascribe earthquakes to the moving of the great tortoise, which bears the *Island* (Continent) on its back. They say he
shakes himself or changes his position."

*Indian Notebooks* VIII, MA 603, P. 286

"Ind. prophets, who say: 'That when the whites have ceased
killing the red man, and got all their lands from them, the great
tortoise which bears this island upon his back, shall dive down
into the deep & drown them all, as he once did before, a "great
many years ago"; and that when he again rises, the Indians shall
once more be put in possession of the whole country.' "

*Indian Notebooks* VIII, MA 603, P. 305

In these selected notes we can see Thoreau's progress between 1852
and 1856 or so. His ambivalent stance toward "unproductive" earth-mound

cultures in Volume VI seems to change to an implied acceptance in Volume VIII of the idea that the very "productive" white race is harmful to North America. His excursions to Maine gave him ample evidence. John Muir would later sound the alarm.

## II

Even though Muir possessed many books relating to American Indian cultures, the majority of his unpublished notes on Indians come from his direct experience; however, some of his notes on Indian wars and Indian oratory come from books.[2] Like Thoreau, the longer Muir knew Indians, the more he grew to appreciate their cultures. The notes which follow are recorded with permission from the Holt-Atherton Pacific Center for Western Studies and are in chronological order. John Muir did not have a set of notebooks specifically dedicated to American Indians; rather, his Indian notes are on fragments of paper and sometimes in typed and revised copy. The dates of his notes are approximate and range from around 1876 to 1910.

[ca. 1876] Wild Sheep hunting nests

One or more Indians hide in nest while companions scour the ridges below knowing that the sheep will seek high peaks
See many of these stone nests on peaks I have climbed.
[ca. 1876] *Modoc War* [See accompanying illustration of Muir's handwritten version on P. 105.]

First hostilities War 1872 & a 2d battle was fought Jan 17th & in both cases the Inds were victorious against enormous odds—
Then the government became anxious to have the matter amicably

settled & gave orders to suspend hostilities & at the same time appointed a Peace Commiss Rev Dr Thomas a methodist clergy man of SF.

Meacham & Applegate belonging to the agency for managing Ind Affairs in Oregon

Gen Canby was appointed to the Supreme Command

After these reached the Modoc country long time spent in arranging a meeting both afraid of treachery

Canby Thomas & Meacham at length met Jack etc

Mr Riddle & his Ind wife went as interpreters

The talk went on when Jack shouted Hetuck Hetuck wh means all ready

Meacham should fight against Schonshin who shot at him 5 times hitting each time the last knockd him over & he remembers nothing afterwards

The troops were in two camps one on the E the other on the W those on E under Col Mason

The Modocs with flag of truce asked for Mason but were told by Leut Sherwood they could not see him there as Sherwood returned he was shot

Muir probably read Alfred B. Meacham's *The Tragedy of The Lava-beds* (Hartford, 1877) and Donald M. Daring's *The Last War—Trail of The Modocs* (Chicago, 1881); this material found its way into the "Early History of the Yosemite" section of *The Mountains of California*.

[ca. 1879–1880]

Ind do not expect treaties but fair play

Think themselves allowed to be protected & punished by the same . . . laws as whites

[ca. 1879–1880]

The Indians complained that the whites taught them how to make the whiskey and furnished them the material and then punished them for using it.

The above notes most certainly relate to Muir's first excursion to Alaska in 1879.

[ca. 1888–1889]

     The following speech of Chief Tenaya's was, of course, used in Muir's first book *The Mountains of California* (1894) in the "Early History of the Yosemite" section. The words which Muir crossed out or added are contained in this transcription.

[Right side of fragment]

It was during this Id [Ind] Expedition that most of the names now in use were given to the falls & rocks of the Valley most of them were selected by Dr. Bunnell [illegible word] of the Ex who has written a <interesting> & valuable history of the discovery of the Valley & of the Ind war wh led to it.

Dr. Bunnell relates that Tenaya after attempting to escape a 2$^d$ time & purposing that he would now be shot. Made the following speech to the Cap Boling "Kill me Sir Cap yes kill me as you killed my son as you would kill all my people if you had the power. Yes Sir America You can now tell your warriors to kill the old chief. You have made my life dark you

[Left side of fragment]

have killed the child of my heart Why not kill the father [.] But when I am dead I will call to my people to come to avenge the death of their chief & his son. You may kill me sir Cap—but you shall not live peace. I will follow in your foot steps I will not leave my home but be with the rocks & <wa> & the waterfalls in the

rivers & winds. Wherever you go I will be with you. You will not
see me but you will fear the spirit of the old chief & grow cold

Muir must have read Dr. Bunnell's *Discovery of the Yosemite* (Chicago,
1880).

[ca. 1890–1899]

The only tree on the prarie worshipped by Inds

I suspect Muir was referring to the cottonwood though he does not mention it by name.

[ca. 1908]

Strange that in so fertile a wilderness we should suffer distress for
the want of a cracker or a slice of bread, while the Indians of the
neighborhood sustained their merry, free life on clover, pine bark,
lupines, fern roots, etcetera, with only now and then a squirrel,
deer or bear, badger, or corn.
　　One of these men was an Indian, and I was interested in
watching his behavior while eating, driving sheep & choosing
a place to sleep at night. He kept a separate camp & how quick
his eye was to notice straggling sheep, and how much better he
seemed to understand the intentions & motions of the flock than
any of the other assistants

This note must have been utilized in part for the writing of *My First Summer in the Sierra* (1911).

[ca. 1908]

I wondered greatly also at the new kinds of men and women; the

Indians belonging to the Menominee and Winnebago tribes who occasionally visited us at our cabin [to get a piece of bread some matches & to sharpen their knives on our grindstone & we had to watch them closely to see that they didn't steal our Ind pony & wondered their knowledge of animals] (The bracketed words were added by Muir to original note.)

[ca. 1908]

The following unpublished typescript with holograph revisions constitutes one of John Muir's sermons in Alaska which the Tlingits greatly appreciated. Words in brackets are either added or crossed out by Muir.

Then I spoke of the brotherhood of man—how we were all children of one father; sketched the characteristics of the different races of mankind, showing that no matter [how far apart their countries were], how they differed in color, [size, language] etc and no matter how <different and how> various the ways in which they got a living, that the white man [& all the people of the world] were essentially alike, <and that all the races of the world were alike; that> we all had ten fingers and ten toes, and in general [our bodies were the same whether] <whether our limbs were the same, although we might have] [white or brown or black different color and speak different languages, > just as though one family of [Tlingit] boys and girls [has been scattered far abroad, formed] <should be sent abroad to different places and> [different tribes] forget their own language, and were so changed in <each form a habit of talking of their own after be> [color by the winds & sunshine of different climates that when after a long] <ing separated so long. The same thing hap> [time they happened to meet they all] <pened all during the journey. Then> [After I had seemed strange to one another.] spoken the Chief always made me address

Chilcat Chief speaking says

"It has always seemed to me while speaking to [fur] traders

<that I have met>, and those who were seeking gold mines, that it was like speaking to a person across a broad stream that was running fast over stones and making so loud a noise, <so> that it was very hard to understand <what> a single word that was said. But now for the first time the white man and the Indian are on the same side of the river, and understand each other."

[ca. 1910]

Of Inds—Spring lie all day with merry jesting from morn til night eating strawberries one meal continuous.

[ca. 1910]

No care is so sure as a good wild solitude. The old sages knew its worth & shamans & prophets & Christ even felt the need of solitude.

In this last fragment we can see an interesting universal religious need for the wilderness from shamans to Christ. Such a core of thought is central not only to John Muir but also to Henry David Thoreau.

Modoc war

Tenth hostilities Nov 1872
+ a 2d battle was fought Jan 17th
& in ____ cases the Inds were victorious
against enormous odds –

Then the government became anxious to have the matter
amicably settled & gave orders to suspend hostilities
& at the same time appointed a Peace Comm—
Rev Dr Thomas a methodist clergyman of S.F.
Meacham & applegate belonging to the agency for
? managing Ind affairs in Oregon
Gen Canby was appointed to the Supreme Command
After these reached the the Modoc country long time
spent in arranging a meeting both afraid of treachery
Canby Thomas & Meacham at length met Jack &c
Mr Riddle & his Ind wife went as interpreters
The talk went on when Jack shouted Hotuck Hotuck
wh means all ready.
Meacham should fight against Schwaskin who
shot at him 5 times hitting ? time the last ?
him over & he remembers nothing afterwards
The ____ men in two camps one on the E the
other on the W those on E under Col Mason
The ____ ____ ____ ____ ____
Mason but were told by Lieut Sherman they
could not see him thus as Sherman returned he
was ____ – ____ ____ ____ ____

# Notes

## CHAPTER I:
## HENRY THOREAU'S INDIAN PATHWAY

1.  Henry David Thoreau, *The Maine Woods*, ed. Joseph J. Moldenhauer (Princeton: Princeton University Press, 1972), P. 69.
2.  Ibid., P. 71.
3.  Henry David Thoreau, *Journal*, eds. Bradford Torrey and Francis H. Allen (Boston: Houghton Mifflin, 1906), X, P. 294.
4.  Henry David Thoreau, *A Week on the Concord and Merrimack Rivers* (Boston: Houghton Mifflin, 1893), P. 69.
5.  See Henry David Thoreau, *Thoreau's Minnesota Journey: Two Documents*, ed. Walter Harding (Geneseo, N.Y.: Thoreau Society Booklet No. 16, 1962). Though Thoreau was dying with tuberculosis during his trip to Minnesota in 1861, he was still deeply inspired by the Indians. Here is his primitivistic account of a Minnesota Sioux dance: "Indians, 30 dance, 12 musicians on drums and others strike arrows against bows. The dancers blow some flutes. Keep good time. Move feet and shoulders, one or both. No shirts. 5 bands there" P. 22.
6.  Thoreau, *Journal*, X, P. 252.

7.   Ibid., IV, P. 400.

8.   Ibid., XI, P. 438.

9.   Ibid., I, P. 444.

10.  Thomas E. Sanders and Walter Peek, *Literature of the American Indian* (Beverly Hills: Glencoe Press, 1973). Subsequent citations will be noted in text with page numbers from this edition.

11.  Roderick Nash, *Wilderness and the American Mind* (New Haven: Yale University Press, 1968), P. 92.

12.  Roy Harvey Pearce, *The Savages of America: A Study of the Indian and the Idea of Civilization* (Baltimore: The Johns Hopkins Press, 1965), Pp. 149–50.

13.  Francis Jennings, *The Invasion of America: Indians, Colonialism, and the Cant of Conquest* (New York: W. W. Norton, 1976), P. 5.

14.  John Aldrich Christie, *Thoreau as World Traveler* (New York: Columbia University Press and American Geographical Society, 1965), P. 231.

15.  Edwin Fussell, Frontier: *American Literature and the American West* (Princeton: Princeton University Press, 1965), P. 349.

16.  Robert F. Sayre, *Thoreau and the American Indians* (Princeton: Princeton University Press, 1977), P. xiii, 146.

17.  Henry Roe Schoolcraft, *Historical and Statistical Information Respecting the History, Condition and Prospect of the Indian Tribes of the United States* (Philadelphia: Lippincott, Grambo & Co., 1851), Part I, P. ix.

18.  Henry David Thoreau, *The Indians of Thoreau: Selections from the Indian Notebooks,* ed. Richard F. Fleck (Albuquerque: Hummingbird Press, 1974), P. 4.

19.  Thoreau, *Indian Notebooks*, VI, P. 111 (from manuscripts at the Pierpont Morgan Library in New York. Volumes I–XI have been given call numbers MA 596–MA 606. Subsequent citations will be noted in text with volume, MA call number, and page number(s).

20.  Lawrence Willson, "The Influence of Early North American History and Legend on the Writings of Henry David Thoreau" (Ph.D. diss., Yale University, 1944), P. 209.

21. Thoreau, *Journal*, X, P. 313.

22. Ibid., XI, P. 437.

23. Thoreau, *The Maine Woods*, P. 289.

24. *Journal*, X, P. 295.

25. Ibid., XIII, P. 144.

26. Thoreau, *The Indians of Thoreau*, P. 67.

27. *Journal*, IX, Pp. 448–49.

28. Henry David Thoreau, "Natural History of Massachusetts," *Excursions* (Boston: Houghton Mifflin, 1893), P. 154.

29. Thoreau, *The Maine Woods*, P. 70.

CHAPTER II:
JOHN MUIR'S HOMAGE TO
HENRY DAVID THOREAU

1. Walter Harding, "Introduction," *Thoreau's Minnesota Journey*, P. i.

2. Ibid., P. 22.

3. It is interesting to note that in an unpublished fragment written ca. 1900 Muir refers to Emerson's correspondence with him in which Emerson said much about Thoreau and he wondered if "anyone in Cal—a young genius—could edit his unpublished MS." Though these letters are apparently lost, it does appear that Emerson hinted to Muir that he should edit the unpublished writings of Thoreau. [Unpublished papers at the Holt-Atherton Pacific Center for Western Studies, hereafter abbreviated as JMP, UOP (John Muir Papers, University of the Pacific).]

4. John Muir, *Our National Parks* (Madison: University of Wisconsin Press, 1981), P. 357.

5. Thoreau, *The Maine Woods*, P. 6.

6. Muir, *Our National Parks*, P. 279.

7. Thoreau, *The Maine Woods*, P. 102.

8. Muir, *Our National Parks*, P. 317.

9. John Muir, *The Life and Letters of John Muir*, ed. William F. Badè

(Boston: Houghton Mifflin, 1923), I, P. 382.
10.  Ibid., II, P. 267.
11.  Ibid., P. 268.

## CHAPTER III:
## JOHN MUIR AMONG THE MAIDU,
## TLINGIT, AND YUP'IK PEOPLE

1.  For the most significant commentary to date on Muir's views on Indians and Yup'iks see Herbert F. Smith, *John Muir* (New York: Twayne Publishers, 1965), Pp. 107–10, 115–21; and Michael Cohen, *The Pathless Way: John Muir and American Wilderness* (Madison: University of Wisconsin Press, 1984), Pp. 184–90. Cohen writes, "one must notice with surprise that Muir didn't look seriously at the possibilities of life suggested by Native American ways" P. 185.
2.  For a good discussion of Muir's spiritual dialogue with his father, see Michael Cohen's essay "Stormy Sermons," in *The World of John Muir* (Stockton: The Holt-Atherton Pacific Center for Western Studies, 1981), Pp. 21–36.
3.  John Muir, *A Thousand-Mile Walk to the Gulf* (Boston: Houghton Mifflin, 1916), Pp. 323–24.
4.  Ibid., P. 343.
5.  Ibid., P. 356–57.
6.  John Muir, *My First Summer in the Sierra* (Boston: Houghton Mifflin, 1916), P. 21.
7.  John Muir, *Travels to Alaska* (Boston: Houghton Mifflin, 1979), P. 61.
8.  Muir, *My First Summer in the Sierra*, P. 153.
9.  Ibid., P. 171.
10.  Ibid., P. 41.
11.  Ibid.
12.  Ibid.
13.  John Muir, *Life and Letters of John Muir*, ed. William Frederick Badè (Boston: Houghton Mifflin, 1923), II, P. 10.

14. Muir, *The Mountains of California*, I, P. 75.
15. John Muir, *John of the Mountains: The Unpublished Journals of John Muir*, ed. Linnie Marsh Wolfe (Madison: University of Wisconsin Press, 1979), P. 315.
16. Muir, *Our National Parks*, P. 336.
17. Muir, *The Story of My Boyhood and Youth*, Pp. 174–75.
18. Thomas J. Lyon, *John Muir* (Boise: Boise State College, 1972), Pp. 14–15.
19. Muir, *My First Summer in the Sierra*. Muir writes, "Indians walk softly and hurt the landscape hardly more than the birds and squirrels, and their brush and bark huts last hardly longer than those of wood rats, while their more enduring monuments, excepting those wrought on the forests by the fires they made to improve their hunting grounds, vanish in a few centuries" Pp. 54–55.
20. Muir, *The Mountains of California*, II, Pp. 254–63.
21. Muir, *Life and Letters of John Muir*, I, Pp. 298–99.
22. John Muir, *Steep Trails*, ed. William Frederic Badè (Boston: Houghton Mifflin, 1916), P. 41.
23. Ibid., Pp. 169–70.
24. Muir, *My First Summer in the Sierra*, P. 89.
25. Ibid., P. 108.
26. Ibid., P. 262.
27. Muir, *Life and Letters of John Muir*, II, P. 22.
28. John Muir, *The Wilderness World of John Muir*, ed. Edwin Way Teale (Boston: Houghton Mifflin, 1954), P. 116.
29. Muir, *My First Summer in the Sierra*, P. 226.
30. Ibid., P. 54.
31. Ibid., P. 74.
32. Ibid., P. 79.
33. Ibid., P. 90.
34. Ibid., P. 116.
35. Muir, *Life and Letters of John Muir*, II, P. 98.
36. Thoreau, *The Maine Woods*, P. 136.
37. Thoreau, *The Indians of Thoreau*, P. 63.

38. Thoreau, *The Maine Woods*, P. 140. Subsequent citations are given a page reference in the text.
39. John Muir, *Travels in Alaska* (Boston: Houghton Mifflin, 1979), Pp. 42–43.
40. Ibid., P. 90.
41. Ibid., P. 91.
42. Ibid., P. 93.
43. Ibid., Pp. 143–44.
44. Ibid., P. 150.
45. Ibid., Pp. 151–52.
46. Ibid., P. 263.
47. Muir, *John of the Mountains*, P. 277.
48. Muir, *Boyhood and Youth*, P. 89.
49. Smith, *John Muir*, P. 104.
50. Muir, *John of the Mountains*, Pp. 271–72.
51. Muir, *Travels in Alaska*, P. 286.
52. Ibid., P. 268.
53. Muir, *The Mountains of California*, I, Pp. 14–15.
54. Muir, *Steep Trails*, P. 342.
55. John Muir, *The Cruise of the Corwin* (Boston: Houghton Mifflin, 1918), P. 126.
56. See Richard F. Fleck, "Thoreau as Mythologist," Research Studies 40 (September 1972), Pp. 195–206.
57. Muir, *Travels in Alaska*, P. 158.
58. Ibid., Pp. 169–70.
59. Ibid., P. 191.
60. Ibid., P. 342.
61. Thoreau, *The Indians of Thoreau*, P. 63.
62. Muir, *The Mountains of California*, I, P. 254.
63. Ibid., II, P. 202.
64. Muir, *Travels in Alaska*, P. 145.
65. Ibid., Pp. 240–41.
66. Ibid., P. 245.

67. Muir, *John of the Mountains*, P. 273.

68. Ibid., P. 315.

69. Samuel Hall Young, *Alaska Days with John Muir* (New York: Revell, 1915), P. 92.

70. Linnie Marsh Wolfe, *Son of the Wilderness: The Life of John Muir* (New York: Knopf, 1945), P. 92.

71. Muir, *Travels in Alaska*, P. 167.

72. Muir, *My First Summer in the Sierra*, P. 226.

73. Muir, *Travels in Alaska*, P. 167.

74. Ibid., P. 285.

75. Ibid., P. 160.

76. Ibid., P. 179.

77. Ibid., P. 239.

78. Ibid., P. 86.

79. Muir, *John of the Mountains*, P. 275.

80. Smith, *John Muir*, P. 121.

81. Muir, *The Cruise of the Corwin*, P. 13. Subsequent citations will be noted by page numbers in text.

82. Among the books in Muir's personal library at Martinez was a copy of Sheldon Jackson's *Thirteenth Annual Report on Introduction of Domestic Reindeer into Alaska* (Washington: Government Printing Office, 1904).

83. Francis Jennings, *The Invasion of America: Indians, Colonialism and the Cant of Conquest* (New York: W. W. Norton, 1976), P. 6.

84. Muir, *Our National Parks*, P. 317.

85. Muir, *John of the Mountains*, P. 277.

86. Muir, *The Mountains of California*, II, P. 291.

87. Stephen Fox, *John Muir and his Legacy* (Boston: Little, Brown and Company, 1981), P. 351.

## APPENDIX

1. This fragmentary essay and other unpublished notes are in addition to those I selected in *The Indians of Thoreau*.

2.  Here follows some significant titles of books relating to American
    Indian and Yup'ik cultures which were in Muir's personal library: G.
    Guernsey Hartnig, *The Polar and Tropical Worlds* (Springfield: C. A.
    Nichols, 1878); Isaac I. Hayes, *The Land of Desolation* (New York:
    Harper & Bros., 1872); Fridtjof Nansen, *The First Crossing of Greenland*
    (New York: Longmans, Green, 1890), 2 vols.; Alpheys Packard, *The
    Labrador Coast* (New York: N. D. D. Hodges, 1891); Francis Parkman,
    *Francis Parkman's Works* (Boston: Little, Brown, 1902), 12 vols.;
    William H. Prescott, *History of the Conquest of Mexico* (Philadelphia:
    David McKay, 1847), 3 vols., and *History of the Conquest of Peru*
    (Philadelphia: David McKay, 1847), 2 vols.; Henry David Thoreau, *The
    Writings of Henry David Thoreau* (Boston: Houghton Mifflin, 1906), 20
    vols. (Muir has written in pencil an index at the back of each Thoreau
    volume with the topic of "Indians" figuring importantly); Egerton
    Ryerson Young, *By Canoe and Dog-Train Among the Cree and Salteaux
    Indians* (London: Charles H. Kelley, 1894).

# A Selective Bibliography

## HENRY DAVID THOREAU

*Primary Sources*

Thoreau, Henry David. *Complete Writings.* 20 vols. Boston: Houghton Mifflin, 1906. *Walden* Edition. This twenty-volume set is slowly being updated and made more definitive and scholarly by Princeton University Press. Because not all of the volumes are available, only the Princeton *Walden* and *Maine Woods* are cited in this study; older editions of the entire Journals and Essays, therefore, serve as primary sources.

——. *Consciousness in Concord: The Text of Thoreau's Hitherto Lost Journal (1840–1841).* Edited by Perry Miller. Boston: Houghton Mifflin, 1958.

——. *Indian Notebooks.* 11 vols. Unpublished manuscripts at the Pierpont Morgan Library, New York (MA 596–606).

——. *The Indians of Thoreau: Selections from the Indian Notebooks.* Edited by Richard F. Fleck. Albuquerque: Hummingbird Press, 1974.

——. *Journal.* Ed. Bradford Torrey. 20 volumes. Boston: Houghton Mifflin, 1906.

——. *The Maine Woods.* Edited by Joseph J. Moldenhauer. Princeton: Princeton University Press, 1972.

——. "Natural History of Massachusetts." *Excursions.* Boston: Houghton Mifflin, 1893.

——. *Thoreau's Minnesota Journey: Two Documents.* Edited by Walter Harding. Geneseo, N.Y.: Thoreau Society Booklet No. 16, 1962.

——. *Walden.* Edited by Lyndon Shanley. Princeton: Princeton University Press, 1971.

——. *A Week on the Concord and Merrimack Rivers.* Boston: Houghton Mifflin, 1893.

## Secondary Sources

Borst, Raymond. *Henry David Thoreau: A Descriptive Bibliography.* Pittsburgh: University of Pittsburgh Press, 1982.

Christie, John Aldrich. *Thoreau as World Traveler.* New York: Columbia University Press, 1965.

Fleck, Richard F. "Thoreau as Mythologist." Research Studies 40 (September 1972), Pp. 195–206.

Fussell, Edwin S. *Frontier: American Literature and the American West.* Princeton: Princeton University Press, 1965.

Harding, Walter Roy. *The Days of Henry Thoreau.* New York: Knopf, 1965.

——. *The New Thoreau Handbook.* New York: New York University Press, 1980.

Jennings, Francis. *The Invasion of America: Indians, Colonialism, and the Cant of Conquest.* New York: W. W. Norton, 1976.

Keiser, Albert. *The Indian in American Literature.* New York: Oxford University Press, 1933.

——. "Thoreau's Manuscripts on the Indians." *Journal of English and Germanic Philology* 27 (April 1928), Pp. 183–99.

Krupat, Arnold. "Ethnohistory and Literature: A Review Article." *Century Review* 23 (1981), Pp. 141–52. (This article reviews Robert F. Sayre's *Thoreau and the American Indians.*)

Lebeaux, Richard. *Thoreau's Seasons.* Amherst: University of Massachusetts Press, 1984.

Nash, Roderick. *Wilderness and the American Mind.* New Haven: Yale University Press, revised and expanded edition, 1983.

Paul, Sherman. *The Shores of America: Thoreau's Inward Exploration.* Urbana: University of Illinois Press, 1958.

Pearce, Roy Harvey. *The Savages of America: A Study of the Indian and the Idea of Civilization.* Baltimore: The Johns Hopkins Press, 1965.

Sayre, Robert F. *Thoreau and the American Indians.* Princeton: Princeton University Press, 1977.

Willson, Lawrence. "The Influence of Early North American History and Legend on the Writings of Henry David Thoreau." Ph.D. diss., Yale University, 1944.

## JOHN MUIR

*Primary Sources*

Muir, John. *The Cruise of the Corwin.* Edited by William Frederic Badè. Boston: Houghton Mifflin, 1918.

——. *John of the Mountains: Unpublished Journals of John Muir.* Edited by Linnie Marsh Wolfe. Madison: University of Wisconsin Press, 1979. Reprint of 1938 edition.

——. *John Muir: Montaineering Essays.* Edited by Richard F. Fleck. Salt Lake City: University of Utah Press, 1997.

——. *The Life and Letters of John Muir.* Edited by William F. Badè. 2 vols. Boston: Houghton Mifflin, 1923.

——. *The Mountains of California.* 2 vols. Boston: Houghton Mifflin, 1916.

——. *My First Summer in the Sierra.* Boston: Houghton Mifflin, 1916.

——. *Our National Parks.* Madison: University of Wisconsin Press, 1981. Reprint of 1916 edition.

——. *Steep Trails.* Edited by William Frederic Badè. Boston: Houghton Mifflin, 1918.

——. *The Story of My Boyhood and Youth.* Boston: Houghton Mifflin, 1916.

——. *A Thousand-Mile Walk to the Gulf.* Boston: Houghton Mifflin, 1916.

——. *John Muir: To Yosemite and Beyond: Writings from the Years 1863–*

*1875*. Edited by Robert Engberg and Donald Wesling. Madison: University of Wisconsin Press, 1980.

———. *Travels in Alaska*. Boston: Houghton Mifflin, 1979. Reprint of 1916 edition.

———. *The Wilderness World of John Muir*. Edited by Edwin Way Teale. Boston: Houghton Mifflin, 1954.

———. *The Yosemite*. New York: The Century Company, 1919.

*Secondary Sources*

Badè, William Frederic. *Life and Letters of John Muir*. 2 vols. Boston: Houghton Mifflin, 1923.

Cohen, Michael. *The Pathless Way: John Muir and American Wilderness*. Madison: University of Wisconsin Press, 1984.

Fox, Stephen R. *John Muir and his Legacy*. Boston: Little, Brown, 1981.

Gifford, Terry. *Reconnecting With John Muir*. Athens: University of Georgia Press, 2006.

Kimes, William F., and Mayime B. *John Muir: A Reading Bibliography*. Palo Alto: William P. Wrenden Books, 1978.

Leopold, Aldo. *A Sand County Almanac*. New York: Oxford University Press, 1949.

Lyon, Thomas J. *John Muir*. Boise: Boise State College, 1972.

Schofield, Edmund A. "Muir and the New England Connection." *The Pacific Historian*, 29 (Summer/Fall 1985), Pp.65–89.

Smith, Herbert F. *John Muir*. New York: Twayne Publishers, 1965.

Wolfe, Linnie Marsh. *Son of the Wilderness: The Life of John Muir*. New York: Knopf, 1945.

Worster, Donald. *The Life of John Muir: A Passion for Nature*. Oxford: Oxford University Press, 2008.

Young, Samuel Hall. *Alaska Days with John Muir*. New York: Revell, 1915.

## AMERICAN INDIANS

Bandelier, Adolph. *Delight Makers*. New York: Harcourt Brace Jovanovich, 1971.

Bunnell, Lafayette. *Discovery of Yosemite*. Los Angeles: G. W. Gerlicher, 1911.

Cather, Willa. *Death Comes for the Archbishop*. New York: Knopf, 1927.

———. *The Professor's House*. New York: Knopf, 1925.

Crantz, David. *History of Greenland*. London, 1767.

Craven, Margaret. *I Heard the Owl Call My Name*. New York: Doubleday, 1973.

Cusick, David. *Sketches of the Ancient History of the Six Nations*. Lockport, N.Y.: Turner & McCollum, 1848.

Daring, Donald M. *The Last War-Trail of the Modocs*. Chicago: Rounds Bros., 1881.

Deloria, Vine, Jr. *Custer Died for Your Sins*. New York: Macmillan, 1969.

Heckewelder, John. *An Account of the History, Manners and Customs of the Indian Nations*. Philadelphia: Transactions of the American Philosophical Society, 1819.

Highwater, Jamake. *The Primal Mind*. New York: Harper & Row, 1981.

Hutchinson, Thomas. *History of the Colony of Massachusetts Bay*. Boston: Thomas and John Fleet, 1769.

Jesuits. *Letters from Missions*. 73 vols. New York: Pageant Book Co., 1959. Facsimile edition.

Levi-Strauss, Claude. *Structural Anthropology*. New York: Doubleday, 1967.

Mackenzie, Alexander. *Voyages from Montreal*. London: Cadell & Davies, 1801.

Mann, Charles C. *1493: Uncovering the New World Columbus Created*. New York: Alfred Knopf, Inc., 2011.

Meacham, Alfred B. *The Tragedy of the Lava-Beds*. Hartford, 1877.

Momaday, N. Scott. *The Way to Rainy Mountain*. Albuquerque: University of New Mexico Press, 1969.

Mountain Wolf Woman. *Mountain Wolf Woman*. Ann Arbor: University of Michigan Press, 1961.

Neihardt, John G. *Black Elk Speaks*. New York: William Morrow, 1932.

Pauketat, Timothy R. *Cahokia: Ancient America's Great City on the Mississippi*. New York: Viking Penguin, 2009.

Pryde, Duncan. *Nunaga*. New York: Bantam Books, 1973.

Sanders, Thomas and Walter Peek, eds. *Literature of the American Indian.*
    Beverly Hills: Glencoe Press, 1973.
Schoolcraft, Henry Roe. *The Historical and Statistical Information Respecting
    . . . the Indian Tribes.* 6 vols. Philadelphia: Lippincott, Grambo,
    1851–60.
Silko, Leslie Marmon. *Yellow Woman and a Beauty of the Spirit.* New York:
    Simon & Schuster, 1996.
Thompson, Stith. *The Folktale.* New York: The Dryden Press, 1946.
Waters, Frank. *The Book of the Hopi.* New York: Viking Press, 1971.
——. *The Man Who Killed the Deer.* Denver: Sage Books, 1942.

# Index